MW00987185

"Christine Aroney-Sine's new book is a pleasure, rejoicing, and play, it celebrates ... ... p....... ... God's exuberant yes to all of creation."

Christine Valters Paintner, author of *The Soul's Slow Ripening*

"Spiritual practice is designed to awaken us to God's presence, but it need not be boring. Aroney-Sine has produced a brave work here, inviting spiritual seekers to become like children—playful, curious, and trusting. With Aroney-Sine's guidance and support you will discover the God who delights in you and unlock a wellspring of joy."

Phileena Heuertz, founding partner of Gravity, a Center for Contemplative Activism, author of *Mindful Silence*

"Once after baptizing some young children, I invited them to splash in the baptismal font and even splash the congregation a bit too. . . . In *The Gift of Wonder*, Christine Aroney-Sine is pointing to those splashing in the water inviting us to do more of the same in order to be more of what God intends for us to be."

Gregory H. Rickel, VIII Bishop of Olympia

"Using stories from the Bible, creative exercises, reflection questions, and her own beautiful poems, Christine addresses the questions of how we can bring joy to God and how we can live out the Christian faith as a journey of discovery. . . . She guides us on pathways to experience God's generous gifts and to grow in contentment and peace in Christ."

Lynne M. Baab, author of *Sabbath Keeping* and *Nurturing Hope*

"Christine Aroney-Sine has always provided a consistently prophetic voice that is edged with intelligence and grace and enfolded in an active spirituality of discipleship. This book continues in that vein. *The Gift of Wonder* takes the reader on a journey of discovery through the integration of goodness, beauty, and truth. A great read."

Alan Hirsch, founder of 5Q Collective and Forge Mission Training Network

"There's a deep desire among so many people I work with as a spiritual director and pastor to connect with God in a new way, to get out of their heads and into their bodies and hearts, to lighten up and play, to experience joy and healing. . . . I have no doubt it will rekindle delight and ignite our sense of wonder for all who engage with it."

Kathy Escobar, copastor of The Refuge, author of *Faith Shift*

"As a pastor committed to the spiritual nurture and formation of my congregation, this book is a dream resource. . . . A robust approach that has something in it for men as well as women. Any individual, group, or leader will find creative inspiration and sustenance to flourish in this book."

Mark Pierson, pastor, worship curator, author of *The Art of Curating Worship*

"*The Gift of Wonder* is a joyful and profoundly serious invitation to get dirty and play with the Creator. This book makes me want to get outside, take out some art supplies, become curious, and experience divine delight! If you are craving a fresh approach to connecting with God, this book will ignite your imagination and inspire you to explore new life-giving practices."

Lisa Scandrette, coauthor of *Belonging and Becoming* and *Free*

"In a culture that values adulthood it will stretch us to explore Jesus' crucial observation that we can only enter the kingdom through childlikeness. To explore that strange reality we'll need some friends on the journey. Christine Aroney-Sine is such a friend, inviting us into the kind of rich, whole-person communal engagement with the God we knew as children. If you join her on this playful, messy, wonder-full adventure, you might never be the same again!"

Mandy Smith, pastor, author of *Making a Mess and Meeting God* and *The Vulnerable Pastor*

"For many, the term 'spiritual disciplines' conjures thoughts of monotonous practices performed alone and by rote, but not for Christine Aroney-Sine. With her usually exuberant style she reimagines the spiritual practices as communal activities that restore the intense joy and unbridled enthusiasm God wants for all followers. *The Gift of Wonder* is indeed a gift for anyone wanting to explore more creative approaches to the spiritual disciplines. The exercises and prayers are worth the price of admission alone."

Michael Frost, author of *Surprise the World* and *Keep Christianity Weird*

"Refreshing and helpful, *The Gift of Wonder* soothed my oft-weary spirit. In our polarized, driven, and consumer-obsessed culture, this book is an invitation into God's creative freedom. Christine not only encourages us to wonder again like a little child, she also gives us practical ways to experience God's delight. From the childlike characteristic of playfulness to trust, she leads us into a rare and grace-filled space of choosing joy."

MaryKate Morse, author and professor

"I trust Christine Aroney-Sine to teach me about wonder because she lives with playful curiosity—discovering beauty in the unexpected and the everyday details of life—and she writes with uncommon eloquence and simplicity."

Mark Scandrette, author of *Belonging and Becoming*, *Practicing the Way of Jesus*, and *Free*

"Christine Aroney-Sine's *The Gift of Wonder* is a book of wisdom and delight! Repeatedly while reading, I found myself grinning and laughing from sheer joy. . . . From philosophical and theological reflection to practical application, Christine shares how to see anew through appreciating God's goodness infused all about us. She gives full permission to *play*—to delight in the Lord's delight of each of us! Read this and then live it; it's that good."

Clint Baldwin, executive director of Word Made Flesh

"Play, pray, plant, paint! Christine Aroney-Sine invites us to recover our childlike sense of wonder. Each page encourages us to pause, to exhale, and to breathe in each moment with holy awe. Aroney-Sine offers wise, practical ways to care for our souls by cultivating gardens all around us. This is lived theology, rooted in the world, mediated through our eyes and ears, hearts, and hands. I'm grateful for such respite and creative renewal."

Craig Detweiler, president of The Seattle School of Theology & Psychology

CHRISTINE ARONEY-SINE

THE GIFT OF WONDER

CREATIVE PRACTICES FOR
DELIGHTING IN GOD

IVP Books
An imprint of InterVarsity Press
Downers Grove, Illinois

InterVarsity Press
P.O. Box 1400, Downers Grove, IL 60515-1426
ivpress.com
email@ivpress.com

InterVarsity Press® is the book-publishing division of InterVarsity Christian Fellowship/USA®, a movement of students and faculty active on campus at hundreds of universities, colleges, and schools of nursing in the United States of America, and a member movement of the International Fellowship of Evangelical Students. For information about local and regional activities, visit intervarsity.org.

All Scripture quotations, unless otherwise indicated, are taken from The Voice™. Copyright © 2012 by Ecclesia Bible Society. Used by permission. All rights reserved.

All the prayers in the chapter epigraphs and a few unattributed prayers in the text are authored by Christine Aroney-Sine. All rights reserved.

Cover design: David Fassett
Interior design: Daniel van Loon
Images: blank paper: © Pinghung Chen / EyeEm / Getty Images
   hummingbird: © Dopeyden / iStock / Getty Images Plus
   rainbow face woman: © Tara Moore / Stone / Getty Images

ISBN 978-0-8308-4653-5 (print)
ISBN 978-0-8308-7158-2 (digital)

Printed in the United States of America ∞

InterVarsity Press is committed to ecological stewardship and to the conservation of natural resources in all our operations. This book was printed using sustainably sourced paper.

Library of Congress Cataloging-in-Publication Data
A catalog record for this book is available from the Library of Congress.

P	25	24	23	22	21	20	19	18	17	16	15	14	13	12	11	10	9	8	7	6	5	4	3	2	1
Y	37	36	35	34	33	32	31	30	29	28	27	26	25	24	23	22	21	20	19						

To all who are learning to laugh

and dance and play with God.

CONTENTS

INTRODUCTION

I choose to enjoy the glory
of the everlasting, ever present One,
To sit and listen
to what delights God's heart.
I choose to breathe in the wonder
of eternal love,
And dance to the rhythm of eternal breath,
listening to the whispers
calling me to slow down and take notice.
I choose to absorb the beauty
of the divine presence,
to delight in the Creator of all things
and relish the delight God takes in me.

Can you imagine a God who dances with shouts of joy, laughs when you laugh, loves to play, enjoys life, and invites us to join the fun? I couldn't until recently.

I grew up with a serious, workaholic type of God who chastised me for not keeping busy twenty-four hours a day, seven days a week. Even when I realized this was not what God was really like, it was hard to change. I felt guilty when I slowed down, took a break, or just went out and had fun. This following Jesus is serious business after all. Like the disciples who tried to chase away the children that came to Jesus,

I couldn't be bothered with frivolous practices where play and laughter disrupted my routines. Gasping in awe and wonder at an opening blossom or a slow-moving caterpillar seemed like a waste of time.

Then one year my early Lenten readings included the verse "Unless you become like children you cannot enter the kingdom of God." These words riveted my attention.

The next day I came across an article by Dr. Stuart Brown, who has dedicated his life to the study of play. We all need play, he believes. It connects us to others, sharpens our minds, and may even help us avoid degenerative diseases like Alzheimer's. "What you begin to see when there's major play deprivation in an otherwise competent adult is that they're not much fun to be around," he says. "You begin to see that the perseverance and joy in work is lessened and that life is much more laborious."[1]

"Seek the kingdom of God above all else," Jesus repeatedly tells his disciples, and this has been the passion of my life. How could play, fun, and the delights of childhood prepare us for this? There was rarely anything childlike about my spirituality or that of my friends and colleagues.

"Let the little children come to me; do not stop them; for it is to such as these that the kingdom of God belongs" (Mark 10:14 NRSV).

HAVE WE DISMISSED THE CHILD WITHIN US AND LOST THE JOY OF LIFE AND THE DELIGHT IN GOD THAT EMERGES WHEN WE PLAY AND LAUGH AND MARVEL AT THE WORLD AROUND US?

Ask kids what they don't like about adults and they say we don't have enough fun. We don't enjoy life enough and we don't enjoy God enough either. To enjoy God more fully and recognize God's delight in us, we must rediscover the world of childhood and unleash the inner child hidden deep in our souls.

I posted this question on Facebook: What are the childlike characteristics that make us fit for the kingdom? I was amazed at the enthusiastic response:

- playfulness

- awe and wonder

- imagination

- curiosity

- love of nature

- compassion

- unconditional trust

These all emerged as childlike qualities that my friends thought were important preparation for the new world Jesus came to introduce us to. Of course, others pointed out that children can also be aggravating, bothersome, and intrusive at the most inopportune moments. Yet as Judy Brown Hull suggests in her insightful book *When You Receive a Child: Reflections on Luke 9:46-48*, even these can be gifts from God that reflect something of the kingdom and the intrusiveness of Jesus as he enters our lives. "Unselfconscious, bothersome, unpredictable—children have another similarity to Jesus: while they are fully human—they do not fit tidily into the totally adult world any better than Jesus did."[2] She provocatively goes on to suggest that this might be because Jesus' reality is closer to that of a child than an adult.

Having listed childlike characteristics that make us fit for the kingdom, responders often commented, "I've never thought about this before." Delighting in fun and laughter as a pathway to enjoying God is something most of us never consider.

We suffer from play deprivation, nature deficit disorder, awe depletion, compassion fatigue, imagination suppression, and more. As a result I think we suffer from God deprivation too.

I am increasingly convinced that rediscovering our inner child is essential for our spiritual health. It has become an important and delightful journey for me and is the central theme of *The Gift of Wonder*.

Awe and wonder, imagination and curiosity connect us to the God who is present in every moment and everything in a way that nothing else can. They enrich our contemplative core and expand our horizons to explore new aspects of our world and our God. Believing in a God who loves to plant gardens with dirty hands and make mud pies to put on the eyes of the blind, or who does happy dances and sings with joy over all of humanity and in fact all of creation has revolutionized my faith.

Ironically, my life has been filled with joy and satisfaction, though I have rarely linked this to my spiritual practices. My childhood in Australia was filled with fun family summer caravan adventures. I studied medicine and delighted in my years as a family physician in New Zealand. In 1981 I joined a fledgling part of Youth with a Mission called Mercy Ships and enjoyed the privilege of establishing a hospital on board the MV *Anastasis*, to perform cleft lip and palate and eye surgeries. Over the twelve years I spent on board, I facilitated surgical outreaches in Mexico, the Caribbean, and Africa. I worked with refugees on the Thai-Cambodian border, in Haiti, and in Ivory Coast. I saw thousands of lives transformed and had the intense joy and satisfaction of knowing my life had made a difference.

After I left the ship, my life took another direction, but I still find intense joy in what I accomplish as an author, speaker, and blogger. Helping people create spiritual pathways that lead them toward a deeper relationship with God is a delight.

My faithful companion over the last twenty-six years of this journey has been my husband, futurist and author Tom Sine. He is constantly researching how our world is changing and how we need to change to be more creative in helping people imagine new possibilities for their lives, churches, and neighborhoods. He loves to cook, walk our dog, and garden with me, and has enthusiastically supported my writing. His insightful and often playful responses to my sharing of new practices have kept me on track throughout.

Tom and I live in a small intentional community in Seattle called the Mustard Seed House. We enjoy a weekly meal and check-in times, which have often provided space for experimenting with the practices I share in this book. We also love to share food from our garden with friends and sometimes strangers from all over the world.

I CHOOSE JOY

My understanding of spiritual disciplines has changed dramatically over the last few years. It continues to change as I delve into the characteristics of childlikeness and rediscover the joy of play and curiosity and awe.

It all began when I asked people, "What makes you feel close to God?" They responded with stories of sitting by the sea, playing with kids, turning the compost pile, washing the dishes, and walking in the local park. Even taking a shower got a mention. Hardly anyone talked about church or Bible study. Most people connect to God through nature, interaction with children, around the dinner table, or in their daily activities. However, they rarely identify these as spiritual practices.

These revelations started me on a journey. Encouraged by contemplative friends, I dived into the liturgical calendar and explored a range of ancient practices like lectio divina and labyrinth walking, which greatly enriched my faith and drew me closer to God.[3] I wrote breathing prayers and liturgies to enhance my personal intimacy with the eternal One. A new depth of delight in God began to emerge. Some of these ideas I shared in my previous book *Return to Our Senses: Reimagining How We Pray*, but my horizons continued to expand.

When I started asking "What do you enjoy about God?" and "What about you gives God joy?" I ventured out beyond the bounds of these ancient but traditional practices to explore creative approaches to prayer, like rock painting and doodling, that stirred my imagination and connected my everyday activities to my relationship with my Creator. I planted prayer gardens and sketched colorful designs as meditative exercises. I had fun with my spiritual practices and invited others to join me on the journey. My inner child was stirring and my soul came alive in ways I never anticipated. I watched friends bubble over with this same enthusiasm for God while engaged in creative activities unlike the traditional practices we grew up with.

The more these practices increased my love for God, the more I wanted to understand what brings joy to God's heart. I incorporated my questions, What do you enjoy about God? and What are you choosing that gives God joy? into my Sunday devotions, where I reflect back on my week and realized that now I needed to reshape my spiritual practices in response to these prompts.

Much to my surprise, many people I talk with are hungry for answers to these same questions yet rarely ask them. Some confess they are not sure anything gives God joy. They see God as a distant, judgmental figure constantly accusing and punishing them for their mistakes. To believe that God is full of joy and enjoys both them and creation is a totally foreign concept. Yet it makes them light up with delight when they begin to understand.

So much of what we learn about spirituality is negative. We believe more in a God of judgment and condemnation than of love, joy, and delight. Following God is about adhering to a long list of things we don't do—no smoking, drinking, dancing, wearing jewelry, or sex before marriage. Alternatively, it is a list of rules that encourage us to color inside the lines and live inside our religious boxes. We live in dread of displeasing God or taking a wrong step that means we can never find God's best for our lives. That God delights in who we are and what we do now is a wonderful but startling revelation for many of us.

Psalm 18:19 tells us we are rescued because God delights in us, and Psalm 147:11 affirms that the eternal One takes pleasure in those who put their hope in God's unfailing love. Even the Westminster Shorter Catechism states that the chief purpose of humanity is "to glorify God and to *enjoy him forever*."

What if finding joy in the divine presence is the greatest way to glorify God and become who God created us to be? What if becoming like a child is the pathway, and what if we reshape our spiritual practices with this in mind?

> WHAT IF FINDING JOY IN THE DIVINE PRESENCE IS THE GREATEST WAY TO GLORIFY GOD AND BECOME WHO GOD CREATED US TO BE?

THE SHAPE OF THIS BOOK

What are the childlike characteristics that bring God joy and make us fit for the kingdom? *is* the question that shapes this book. Asking it in my own life opened hidden doorways for me, a little like Lucy in C. S. Lewis's classic *The Lion, the Witch and the Wardrobe*. She steps through the wardrobe into the magical world of Narnia, where animals speak and creation dances. She gazes on it with awe and wonder and a delight, which grew as she met its inhabitants and burst into life as the great king Aslan approached.

My own magical doorway took me into a mystical world of awe and wonder walks, joy-spot sightings, nostalgia trips, compassion games, and playdate adventures. I relearned the arts of gratitude and curiosity, as well as the delight of living in the present rather than the past or future. Here too creation speaks, relationships are strengthened, and my love for the God revealed in Jesus Christ has taken on new vibrancy and depth, which I hope to share with you.

This book will teach you to pay attention to childlike characteristics that shape us into kingdom people. Each chapter addresses one characteristic we need to embrace:

- delight in God
- playfulness
- sharing our stories
- imagination
- curiosity
- awe and wonder
- love of nature
- the ability to live in the present
- gratitude
- compassion
- hospitality
- the intrigue of looking with fresh eyes
- trust

The Gift of Wonder explores how to reshape our spiritual practices so that giving God joy and drawing closer to our loving Creator becomes their primary purpose. The last chapter is on trust. Here we will braid together the lessons from previous chapters into a strong, unbreakable cord that revitalizes our faith.

Chapters include stories of others who follow this path. I am not the only one exploring new and meaningful approaches to spiritual disciplines or experimenting with creative ways to bring joy to God as I express faith. Nor am I the only one relishing a growing delight in God as a result. Many people I know are creating fresh ways to pray, imaginatively reshaping and adapting time-honored liturgical practices to their current lifestyles and making them uniquely their own. They are hungry for vital faith but bored with traditional practices. They are exploring experiential approaches to spirituality that integrate everyday activities into their faith. In the process they, like me, are discovering the delights of childlike faith that draws us into God's kingdom.

Each chapter concludes with a creative exercise that invites you to awaken your inner child. These exercises encourage you to apply your newfound knowledge to your faith as you reflect on what you have read. Some draw on fun-filled childhood activities like coloring, doodling, and reading children's books, which reduce our stress and free us to enter more fully into our enjoyment of God. Others adapt practices that have existed in the church for centuries, like contemplation and labyrinth walking. Still others are based on totally new ideas of how to practice our faith and draw close to our delightful God.

Build a toolkit. Start by gathering

- a notebook or journal
- some crayons
- colored pens, pencils, or paints
- a coloring book
- your favorite children's book
- your camera (or phone) if you enjoy taking photos
- your favorite musical instrument
- your Bible

This toolkit incorporates elements that appeal to most learning styles. What else should you add? Do you already use creative tools that cater to your learning style? Are you a visual learner inspired by images, maps, or graphic designs? You might like to add photos. Perhaps you are an auditory learner stirred by music, podcasts, lectures, and listening situations. You might want to include a drum or singing bowl. If you learn best through words, loving to take notes and read, a journal and some of your favorite books might be your primary tools. Tactile learners who love hands-on projects and figure things out by putting them together might like to add whittling tools, a puzzle, or your knitting.

JOURNEY WITH OTHERS

This is not a journey you want to attempt alone. Recruit a group of fellow searchers as companions. Plan weekly meetings where you can give each other permission to have some fun, become like children, and explore the creative exercises together.

Parker Palmer in *A Hidden Wholeness* comments, "To understand true self—which knows who we are in our inwardness and whose we are in our larger world—we need both the interior intimacy that comes with solitude and the otherness that comes with community. . . . Together they make us whole, like breathing in and breathing out."[4]

Part of what I love about community is the way we spark each others' creativity and imagination. Creativity gives birth to more creativity. Shared awe and wonder grow until they fill the horizon. Sharing our stories ignites creativity, sparking something new within us *and* others. Like a wildfire spread by the wind, creativity jumps from place to place, bursting into flame, burning away the old to make way for the new. "And in the sharing we experience the joy a second time."[5]

Each creative exercise provides special instructions for group interaction. Reflect on your responses to the exercises at the end of the chapters. Create new practices together. Laugh, eat, and have fun together.

So let us choose the joy of unleashing our inner child today. Let us begin the adventure of reshaping our spiritual practices to delight in God and appreciate the delight that God takes in us.

DELIGHT YOURSELF IN GOD

Stop, pray and listen.
Open yourself to the eternal One
present all around.
Take time to notice the markers
of God's abiding presence
and rejoice in God's enduring acts.
Pause to acknowledge
how far we have come
on this journey toward life.
Hold on to the signs
that nudge us onward along the path
that leads into the loving heart of the One
who is making all things new.

What about me gives God joy? When I first asked myself this question, my mind went blank. I sat in silence for five minutes trying to think of one thing that I thought God liked about me. I knew God loved me, after all love is the essence of who God is. To love is God's nature, almost, one might think, God's duty. That God might actually enjoy who I am and love me because of that enjoyment rather than out of a sense of obligation was a new concept.

So I pulled out a blank sheet of paper and some gel pens and began to create. I wrote the words "What about me gives God joy?" in large letters with a colored pen. I paused, recited the words, picked up a different colored pen and wrote over my first set of letters. One color followed another until my words were a rainbow of delightful images. Each time I wrote the words, I recited them slowly to myself.

Finally, I sat and prayerfully looked at my lettering. *What about me gives you joy, Lord?* I asked again. *I am fearfully and wonderfully made, and God delights in me,* I thought. I pulled out my Bible and read Psalm 139.

Suddenly God's presence embraced me in a tangible way I had never experienced before. I was reminded of Eric Liddell, Scottish Olympic gold medal winner in the 1920s whose life was highlighted in the film *Chariots of Fire.* At one point he tells his sister, "[God] made me fast. And when I run I sense His pleasure."

What do I enjoy doing that makes me sense God's pleasure? I pondered as the joy of God bubbled up inside me. It was as though God had been waiting for me to ask this all my life.

The words started to flow:

"I sense God's pleasure when I let go of my busyness, sit quietly and allow God's presence to permeate my being and lodge in my soul.

I sense God's pleasure when my creative juices flow and I express my love for God by painting rocks, planting contemplative gardens, and writing prayers.

I sense God's pleasure when my husband and I sit together in the evening and take time just to enjoy each other.

I sense God's pleasure when I pull weeds, plant, and prune in the garden, even when I just admire its beauty.

I sense God's pleasure when I help others along the pathway toward a more intimate relationship with God and enable them to become more of whom God created them to be.

I sense God's pleasure when I speak out against injustice and oppression and commit myself to wholeness, peace, and shalom.

God doesn't just love me, God delights in me and who I am created to be, I realize. It was a revolutionary and transforming idea.

I now use this exercise regularly when I journal on Sundays. I might focus on the day or past week. Sometimes I reflect back over several months or a whole year. It is wonderful to be reminded of what God delights in about me and how my daily choices can increase that delight. It has brought a joy and closeness to my relationship that I never anticipated.

The prayer at the beginning of this chapter came out of this process. It encourages me to slow down and notice while focusing my attention on my growing understanding of what it means to not only delight in God but to recognize God's delight in me.

What do you enjoy doing that makes you sense God's pleasure?

According to Andrew Newberg and Mark Robert Waldman, "the human brain is uniquely constructed to perceive and generate spiritual realities."[1] I suspect this innate spirituality is part of our DNA, deeply rooted in our identity as children of God. Perhaps it is also because this is where our joy in life is rooted. We are designed to draw pleasure from our spiritual practices and interactions with God.

> WHAT DO YOU ENJOY DOING THAT MAKES YOU SENSE GOD'S PLEASURE?

When we pray, our brains are changed. Meditation makes us more compassionate and caring toward others. Worshiping together activates pheromones in our bodies that strengthen community. Faith tempers anxiety and fear. We are created to live in love, enjoy God, and bring joy to God not alone but as a united global family.

No wonder even nonreligious people crave spirituality. No wonder our exploration of spiritual practices has the potential to light up our brains and delight our hearts as they open doorways into God's eternal world of love and peace.

Unfortunately, we often allow what someone else enjoys, rather than what delights us, to shape our practices, and that doesn't always bring joy to us or God. Consequently, many lose their way and find no joy in the journey.

"Spiritual but not religious" is used to describe a growing number of people, especially young people for whom church and traditional spiritual practices and worship are no longer satisfying. Many guiltily confess they experience more joy and feel closer to God in nature, yoga, social entrepreneurship, or community service than they do in their Sunday worship service. Some quietly leave church because they get little help in connecting these joy-filled moments to their faith. Others embrace contemplative practices such as lectio divina, labyrinths, and meditation, but receive little encouragement to venture into new pathways. Church activities like prayer stations can tap into this hunger and provide inspirational and experiential practices to bring to our traditional services. Other personal practices, from poetry, knitting, or whittling while praying and meditating while gardening, show an emerging world of creativity for individuals and communities of faith that bring joy to their lives and to the heart of God.

We are all unique expressions of our loving God. How we relate to God says something of who we are and of who God is. Yet we are rarely encouraged to explore or nurture that uniqueness and how it can draw us into God's presence.

What do you enjoy about God? and What are you choosing that gives God joy? should be at the forefront of our spiritual exploration. When I suggested this to a friend who attends Bethel Church in Redding, California, she told me that this church has a similar understanding and encourages people to ask God, *What do you enjoy about me, Lord?* or even *What do you think about me, Lord?* They then prayerfully write down whatever comes to mind.

REJOICING THE HEART OF GOD

My greatest joy as a medical doctor was the thrill of delivering babies. I gazed in awe as the baby's head emerged and held my breath as I waited for its first cry. I delighted in holding the small, squirming body in my hands and loved watching the tears of joy stream down the mother's face as I passed the newborn infant to her. The grin spreading across the father's face made me want to dance and shout with the thrill of it all. I imagine God looked over my shoulder with this same delight.

I experienced that same joy when I was reborn as a child of God. I still vividly remember sitting on a rock on a warm summer's afternoon looking out over the Lane Cove River in Sydney. As I bowed my head in prayer, the fragrance of gum leaves filled my senses, and my heart sang to the joyful shouts of parrots and the deafening sound of cicadas. My world exploded in joy.

In the weeks that followed I really did feel as though I had been born again. Everything was new and fresh. I couldn't stop smiling. Awe and wonder, a glimpse of the magical kingdom of God, surrounded me. No wonder Jesus told Nicodemus, "No one can see the kingdom of God unless they are born again" (John 3:3 NIV). To enter the kingdom we must be reborn into the delights of childhood.

The disciples get the same response when they ask what it will take for them to enter the kingdom of heaven: "Truly I tell you, unless you change and become like little children, you will never enter the kingdom of heaven. Therefore, whoever takes the lowly position of this child is the greatest in the kingdom of heaven" (Matthew 18:3-4 NIV).

On another occasion Jesus becomes elated and prays with joy, "Thank you, Father, Lord of heaven and earth. Thank you for hiding Your mysteries from the wise and intellectual, instead revealing them to little children" (Luke 10:21).

It is easy for us to dismiss this as a metaphor, even if our conversion experiences brought a sense of childlike exuberance. However the great Swiss theologian Hans Urs von Balthasar suggests that we need to take it literally. He believes that our alienation from God has buried in oblivion much of who God created us to be. He sees conversion as a rebirth into a truly childlike mentality in order to participate in God's kingdom. "This

over mistaken notion of separation

True Christ-nature (childlike) always present in us and all creation. No separation. No falling away. We "merely"

16 | THE GIFT OF WONDER *need to awaken from the illusion of separation.*

demands of Jesus' listener a reawakening to his true origin, to which he has turned his back, a spiritual turnabout (unless you convert and become like children) that will enable him to become aware of himself."[2]

Balthasar sees childlikeness particularly in terms of dependency. Only in once more recognizing our total reliance on God can we enter the kingdom.

However, I think it goes much further than that. God's kingdom is a new world with a totally new culture, new language, customs, values, and purpose. To delight in God, enjoy God's eternal world, and enter the fullness of life it offers, we must be reborn and learn to delight in this very different world where the language, culture, and customs are summed up in the words, "You shall love—'love the Eternal One your God with everything you have: all your heart, all your soul, all your strength, and all your mind'—and 'love your neighbor as yourself'" (Luke 10:27).

Love permeates everything God is and does. It entwines our souls. It should be "what fires our imaginations and schedules our time. It should" determine what breaks our hearts and what we celebrate with joy.

What unveils this love in us? Not our intelligence, theological knowledge, or spiritual maturity but our childlikeness—curiosity and questioning, and willingness to make mistakes, live with ignorance, delight in stories, love nature, have fun playing, and be blind to color, creed, age, and social strata in those we associate with. This rejoices the heart of God and makes us fit for the kingdom. So why don't our spiritual practices always reflect that?

I have spent many years traveling in countries not my own, feeling uncomfortable in the cultures, unable to understand the language. Even now, though I have lived in America for twenty-five years, I struggle to understand some aspects of the culture. It is hard. It's not just that my accent is different or that I interpret words differently. At times I feel as though I am on a different wavelength. My humor falls flat. The fun things of my childhood have no meaning. I have had to be born again in order to fit in.

No wonder we need to be reborn to enter the kingdom of God. To learn this language of love, trust in this God of love, and live into God's culture of love, we must enter as infants and move slowly toward childlike maturity. Children learn new languages and cultures far better than we adults do.

It was reading *The Book of Joy* by the Dalai Lama and Desmond Tutu that really connected me to God's joy and the rebirthing pathway I should follow to embrace it. These two amazing men, who survived more than fifty years of what could have been soul-crushing violence and exile, are some of the most joyful, loving people on the planet. "Joy is a way of approaching the world," says the Archbishop Tutu.[3] Our greatest joy, he contends, is when we seek to do good for others, share generously, and show compassion. The more we turn toward others, the more joy we experience; and the more joy we experience, the more we can bring joy to others. The goal is not just to create joy for ourselves but as the archbishop poetically phrased it, "to be a reservoir of joy, an oasis of peace, a pool of serenity that can ripple out to all those around you."[4]

My own spiritual journey toward a God who delights in life, love, and beauty also emerged in a place of deep pain about thirty-five years ago. Two months working on the Thai-Cambodian border with Khmer refugees who had fled the Pol Pot regime in Cambodia turned my faith upside down. Starving kids died in my arms. Their mothers told horrifying stories of rape, violence, and atrocity. *Does God care? If so where is the God of love I believe in, and what does this God expect of me in the midst of these horrors?*

Following this painful experience, I began exploring the biblical concept of shalom and God's desire for the restoration of the wholeness, flourishing, and prosperity of the original creation. As I melded this into my understanding of Sabbath, my desire to make life choices that brought joy to God really began to come into focus and reshape my spiritual practices.

So looking back. I think evolution is pulling us to for word - toward redemption of creation.

In his book *The Sabbath*, Jewish philosopher Abraham Heschel tells of how ancient rabbis puzzled over Genesis 2:2, "On the seventh day God finished his work," which implied to them that there was an act of creation on this day too. They concluded that what was created on the seventh day was "harmony, peace and repose—*menuha*—the world of shalom, wholeness and abundance, the world as God intended it to be."[5] Then God looks at this world and proclaims, "It is very good." Theologian Norman Wirzba suggests that what is expressed here is God's excitement and enthusiasm for what is being created. God finds the whole of creation to be not only good but delightful, "the occasion for intense and sustained joy."[6]

To top it off, God digs a garden, "*a place of utter delight*" (Genesis 2:8) and creates humans as its caretakers. God not only delights in creation but loves to share that world with us and rejoices over our appreciation of its beauty and our acceptance of our role as its stewards. My vivid imagination has God walking through the garden with Adam and Eve pointing out plants, insects, and furry creatures to them saying, "Did you notice this one, see how perfectly it fulfills its part in my plan? I had such fun creating it."

Can you imagine the grief God must have felt at our disobedience? We no longer delighted in our Creator but hid in fear instead. We no longer saw God as delighting in us but viewed the Eternal One as an authoritarian, judgmental, punishing God we could never please. We no longer found joy in the stewardship of this beautiful creation either but saw our labors as toil and struggle, and ourselves as conquerors rather than preservers.

Fortunately, the gospel story offers us hope. In *A New Heaven and a New Earth* Richard Middleton says,

> Many recent studies of the garden of Eden in Genesis suggest that this garden, in its relationship to the rest of the earth,

functions as an analogue of the holy of holies in the tabernacle or the Jerusalem temple. The garden is the initial core location of God's presence on earth; this is where God's presence is first manifest, both in giving instructions to humanity (2:15-17) and in declaring judgement (3:8-19). The garden is thus the link between earth and heaven, at least at the beginning of human history. The implication is that as the human race faithfully tended this garden or cultivated the earth, the garden would spread, until the entire earthly realm was transformed into a fit habitation for humanity. But it would thereby also become a fit habitation for God.[7]

What if the goal of our spiritual disciplines was to restore the intense joy and enthusiasm God experienced on the seventh day of creation? Imagine what our lives would look like if our deepest delight was to transform ourselves, our neighbors, and the earth until all becomes once again not just a fitting habitation for humanity but also for God.

According to Heschel, "The essence of the world to come is Sabbath eternal."[8] Sabbath is not a rest of exhaustion but of delight. When the Jews looked forward to the Sabbath, they looked beyond the pain of a broken world to the glimpses of wholeness in the past week. The greeting that ushered in the Sabbath day, "*Shabbat Shalom*," basically meant, "May you live in anticipation of the day when God makes all things whole again." This was the culmination of their week, a preview of the world in which Sabbath eternal would reemerge and all God's creation would live in harmony, peace, and abundance.

> WHAT IF THE GOAL OF OUR SPIRITUAL DISCIPLINES WAS TO RESTORE THE INTENSE JOY AND ENTHUSIASM GOD EXPERIENCED ON THE SEVENTH DAY OF CREATION?

Jesus and his announcing of God's new creation fulfills this dream. As I comment in my previous book *Godspace: Time for Peace in the Rhythms of Life*:

> No wonder he healed on the Sabbath and constantly criticized the legalisms and restrictive rules the Pharisees inflicted on the people, robbing them of their joy and freedom. He wasn't downplaying the importance of Sabbath as a holy day, he was showing the Jews what Sabbath was meant to be—a glimpse into the wholeness and abundance of a *shalom* future when all will be healed, fed and provided for.[9]

When I look at Jesus, I see a man with childlike enthusiasm. He loved life, relished the beauty of God's creation, played with children, and enjoyed friendships enthusiastically. I see him rejoicing as he feeds and heals people and breaks down barriers of power and injustice. As I watch him walk through Palestine with his friends, it is not just a love of freedom, justice, and generosity that I sense God loves. More playful images come to mind. *God loves to have fun and surprise people*, I conclude as Jesus turns water into wine at a wedding. *God enjoys a good meal*, I surmise as I watch Jesus eat with his friends. *God loves to celebrate and party*, I imagine as I see Jesus going up to Jerusalem for the Jewish feasts.

What difference would it make to our spiritual practices if we approached life with childlike enthusiasm and made modeling glimpses of God's shalom world our goal? How would we reorder our lives if we started each day by asking, *What does God enjoy about me, and what could I do today to bring joy to God?* How would we reshape our spiritual practices if we saw them as tools to draw us closer to God, to each other, and to God's beautiful world? I suspect this would cast a different view of the day ahead and for the purpose of what we do.

PRACTICE

Choose Joy

This first exercise is adapted from the prayer of examen, a contemplative practice created by Ignatius of Loyola in the sixteenth century to examine our days, detect God's presence, and discern God's purposes.[1] He referred to those elements of our day that bring us closer to God as *consolations* and those that distance us from God as *desolations*. I reshaped this concept to focus on our enjoyment of God and God's joy in us. This is a great way to start our journey into the delight of God.

Gather a blank sketch book or journal and some colored crayons, pens, or pencils. Write "I choose joy" on the first blank page in bold colored letters.

Each night for the next week prayerfully think back over your day.

- What did you enjoy doing? What made you smile, laugh, dance, or shout out loud for joy today?
- How did you respond to these joyful moments?

Use your colored pencil to decorate the words you wrote. If you feel inclined, embellish your reflections with sketches, photos, or words of praise. Perhaps you would like to dance around your room in response or "make a joyful noise" on a drum or guitar.

Imagine God entering into your joy.

- In what ways did these joyful moments make you sense God's pleasure and draw you closer to God?
- In what ways did they draw you closer to others?
- What creative impulses or responses did they stir within you?
- What could you do tomorrow to cultivate and grow that joy?

Name the tensions.

- What destroyed your joy today and made you feel distant from God?

Joy happens in the body. God permeates all creation including our Bodies. When we experience real joy, how might that be a God moment?

- What distanced you from others and perhaps destroyed their joy?
- What adjustments could you make to overcome the tensions and restore your joy?

Reward yourself.

Each evening, reward yourself for the creative responses that enhanced your joy. Give yourself a special treat for each tension that turned into a joy-filled moment where you sensed God's pleasure: eat a chocolate, listen to your favorite song, spend a few extra moments playing with your children. Laugh at yourself. Toast yourself for being a person who is able to overcome tension and create joy spots. As you laugh I hope that you will sense God's approval of your contemplation.

At the end of the week take extra time to relax and look back over your week.

- What gave you the greatest joy?
- What do you think gave the greatest pleasure to God?
- What could you do this coming week to expand your own joy and the pleasure you brought to God?

As a reward, plan a trip to a place you enjoy—an art gallery or museum; a garden you love; the beach or mountains; the oldest, most beautiful, or unusual building in your town; the local nursery or fabric store. Have some fun, enjoy life, and enjoy God.

HAVE FUN WITH YOUR FRIENDS

If you are meeting as a group, get each person to share their joys and distractions from the week. Talk about their responses and where God seemed close or distant. Laugh together. Have some fun. Reward the person who related the most joy-filled moments with a prize or special treat. Give another reward for the one whose response made you laugh the most.

Reflect on your time together. Where did you as a group sense God's pleasure? What new practices might come out of this experience?

OPEN YOURSELF TO AWE
AND WONDER

How delightful it is
to live in a place of beauty,
to share the joy of life
with the great I AM.
How delightful it is
to see the birds hovering overhead,
and hear the whispering wind
rustling through the trees.
I breathe in the rhythm of God's world,
the ebb and flow of seasons,
the fading of day's bright light
into night's embrace.
I dance for joy
surrounded by God's grandeur
and open my senses to wonder and awe.
I sit content in the glory of God's embrace
and absorb the fragrance of God's loving presence.

The 2017 solar eclipse was an awe-inspiring event in Seattle, and I was caught up in the thrill and excitement of it. I watched as the sky darkened to blue and then black. Crescent-shaped sunspots danced under the trees, slowly narrowing until they disappeared into the darkness. I squinted through my eclipse glasses awed by the same diminishing crescent of light that was the sun slipping behind the moon. An eerie silence fell over the neighborhood. Then a small sliver of light reappeared, growing until the sun once more shone as a magnificent golden orb. Kids danced. Their parents cheered. We all burst into tears and hugged each other.

There was something both unsettling and exhilarating about it. We were overcome by the feeling of being part of something immense, beautiful, and much bigger than ourselves. It didn't just hit our eyes with its wonder; it penetrated our souls and pierced deep into our spirits.

It is sad that it takes a rare event like this to awaken awe and wonder in us. So much of what seems miraculous to a child, adults try to explain away with rational, scientific knowledge, often destroying the mystery, awe, and wonder in the process. We no longer dance and sing exuberantly before God like David did, but are more inclined to react like his David's wife, Micah, who, as so often happens with those who no longer live in the world of awe and wonder, despises his demonstrative joy (2 Samuel 6:16).

Wonder is a beautiful gift from God. Magical, awe-inspiring feelings change our approach to life.

> Awe imbues people with a different sense of themselves, one that is smaller, more humble and part of something larger. Our research finds that even brief experiences of awe, such as being amid beautiful tall trees, lead people to feel less narcissistic and entitled and more attuned to the common humanity people share with one another. In the great balancing act of our social lives, between the gratification of self-interest and a concern for others, fleeting experiences of awe redefine the self in terms of the collective, and orient our actions toward the needs of those around us.[1]

Father Greg Boyle, in *Barking to the Choir*, suggests it isn't just nature that gives us this sense of awe. We can embrace the marginalized with a sense of awe too. He comments beautifully: "Awe softens us for the thunder glance of God, then enables us to glance at others in just the same way."[2]

Unfortunately, the research also suggests that we are awe-deprived. We sit behind computers, not beside trees. We rarely visit art galleries, live music, theater, and museums. Even schools are dismantling their arts and music programs. Unfettered time outdoors is being cut for more résumé-building activities. Our bodies, our faith, and our concern for others all suffer as a result. Some of the leading researchers looking at this subject believe that "awe deprivation has had a hand in a broad societal shift" making us "more individualistic, more self-focused, more materialistic and less connected to others."[3] To reverse this trend, they suggest that we all need to experience more everyday awe, and actively look for and take notice of what gives us goose bumps, be it in looking at trees, night skies, cloud patterns, or children playing.

The Bible is full of childlike awe and wonder. We see it in Moses as he praises the great Creator of the universe in his goose bump producing song in Deuteronomy 10:14, 17:

> To the LORD your God belong the heavens, even the highest heavens, the earth and everything in it. . . . For the LORD your God is the God of gods and Lord of lords, the great God, mighty and awesome, who shows no partiality and cannot be bribed. (NIV)

We hear it in David's exclamation of praise of creation in Psalm 65:8:

> The whole earth is filled with awe at your wonders;
> where morning dawns, where evening fades,
> you call forth songs of joy.

I suspect it as also this type of awe and wonder that had him dancing before God as he helped return the ark of the covenant to Jerusalem (2 Samuel 6:14).

Jesus too lived in the world of joyful, childlike awe and mystery. We sense it in his zest for life and the wonderful way he communicates with God, inspiring his disciples to crave new joy-filled ways to pray. We see it in Jesus' enthusiasm for creation and his encouragement to his followers to go out and look closely at the birds and think about the wild lilies (Luke 12:27). We experience it in his embrace of kids, enjoyment of meals, and passion for healing and wholeness. Our daily experience of life, God, and God's world are meant to inspire us with the awe and wonder of childhood.

According to John Pridmore in his fascinating book *Playing with Icons: The Spirituality of Recalled Childhood*, in which he analyzes a rich variety of people's memories of their childhoods, our decline in capacity to notice the miracles around us as we grow older is "a failure of the spirit as well as the senses."[4] He argues that by the time we become adults we lose our child's eye and no longer experience everyday objects with all our senses or capture them in their true light because they are now familiar and commonplace. It takes a rare event like a solar eclipse to stir within us the spirit-touching awe and wonder kids experience every day.

Pridmore points out that when Jesus drives out the traders and money changers in the temple, then heals the blind and the lame, the authorities get angry but the children sing and dance because "for Jesus it is the children alone who see the significance of the *thaumasia*, the wonderful things he is doing."[5] Jesus reminds the authorities that "out of the mouths of infants and nursing babies you have prepared praise" (Matthew 21:16 ESV).

"Rings of children circled round and sang, 'Hosanna to the Son of David'" (Matthew 21:15). The children alone recognized the wonder of what he did. Have you ever noticed that? If you say no you are not alone. No one else I mentioned this to has either. Not only have we lost our ability to appreciate awe and wonder, we no longer notice those, especially the children, who do.

In our awe-deprived lives, I suspect we also miss the awesome significance of the gift of loaves and fishes from a small boy to feed

Everything a miricle

OPEN YOURSELF TO AWE AND WONDER | 27

thousands (John 6:8-10). The disciples are overwhelmed with the impossible burden of providing food when there is none. They have no room for miracles. I wonder, did the children come as a crowd with their little friend and his gift eager to see what Jesus would do? Did they cheer and jump with excitement while their parents tried to push them away and keep them quiet? Only the children truly saw the wonder of who Jesus was and believed he could perform a miracle to feed all of them with this meager offering.

In my early days on board the MV *Anastasis* I had a similar experience. We were stuck in Greece trying to resurrect this old ship, with very little money and fewer resources. During a forty-day fast to seek God's guidance for the future, we met each morning for prayer in a room that looked out over the Mediterranean Sea.

One day toward the end of our fast we looked outside and noticed silver streaks flashing in the sunlight. "The fish are jumping" someone called, and we raced outside. Fish were jumping out of the sea and stranding themselves on the beach. We grabbed pots and pans and wheelbarrows, excitedly collecting 8,301 fish flapping furiously as they gasped for air. We danced, we sang, and we exalted like kids in the God who had provided in this unexpected and awe-inspiring way.

When was the last time you experienced a sense of wonder at the world around you or sat in awe of God's greatness? When was the last time you jumped with excitement and shouted your praises to God, believing that God still performs miracles of provision and healing? Perhaps it is time to reenter the awe-inspiring world of

WHEN WAS THE LAST TIME YOU EXPERIENCED A SENSE OF WONDER AT THE WORLD AROUND YOU OR SAT IN AWE OF GOD'S GREATNESS?

childhood where everything is a miracle. Maybe it is time to rethink our spiritual practices to make this possible.

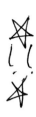

The first key to recovering awe and wonder is to allow for silence. Not the silence that comes from an absence of noise but *silentium*, the silence of attentiveness toward God. Only *silentium* provides a quiet space for our souls, allows our imaginations to flourish, and opens us to awe of our amazing God. This form of quietness is not easy to find because it isn't about place but attitude. *Silentium* encourages us to slow down, set aside the distractions of minds, hearts, and daily activities to draw from the quiet inner center to commune with the spirit of God in a special way.

ENTER THE SILENCE

The contemplative practice of lectio divina with its invitation to this kind of listening silence opened my soul to awe and wonder once more. Lectio divina is an ancient prayer technique once widespread in Christian practice. Its popularity is increasing once again as practitioners find it unveils underlying spiritual rhythms in daily life.

In her book *Lectio Divina: The Sacred Art*, which is the most helpful book I have read on lectio divina, Benedictine oblate Christine Valters Paintner describes lectio as "a practice of being present to each moment in a heart-centered way. Our memories, images, and feelings become an important context for experiencing God's voice active in us, and we discover it when we pray from our hearts. Those words moving through us break open God's invitation to us in this moment of our lives and call us to respond."[6]

Lectio invites us to shut out the distractions of inner and outer noise and sit quietly in the presence of God. It encourages us to relish and savor not just the meaning of the verses we read but also the new and inspiring revelations of God they bring to our days. I love the way that it invites us to center ourselves on God and listen contemplatively for what God's Spirit might say.

There are four movements to lectio divina that take fifteen to thirty minutes to complete.

(1) We begin with *lectio*, a reverential listening in a spirit of silence and awe. Settle into your prayer space, let go of your distractions, and open yourself to the mystery of prayer. Read through your Bible verse slowly several times, attentively and gently listening for a word or phrase that stands out or, as Paintner describes it, "shimmers" as God's word for you today.

(2) In the second movement, *meditatio*, we welcome what stirs as a form of inner hospitality. This is where we speak with God and allow God's Word to affect us at our deepest levels. We

> move the words into [our] heart and allow them to be broken open. . . . When we enter into the wide open space of our hearts and imaginations, we give room for connections to emerge, to notice the resonances this word or phrase has with our own experience. There is a spirit of playfulness that is set free as we enter into the text with openness. When we "play" with the words, we allow ourselves to stretch beyond our own assumptions and rules about what something means.[7]

Read the text again and savor the word or phrase that caught your attention. Allow it to unfold in your imagination. Savor it. What memories, feelings, sensations, and images does it evoke? Perhaps a special meal, with all its flavors, aromas, and joyful celebration comes to mind. How does the text interact with your inner world of concerns and ideas?

In the third movement, *oratio*, we respond in ways that connect the passage to our everyday lives. The intimacy of opening our hearts to God and listening for what stirs within us encourages us to be more active and engaged in our world. We share God's ache for a hurting world. We rejoice in God's delight in the beauty of creation. Prayer bubbles up spontaneously from within and awe and wonder emerge as our hearts are touched and God draws close. It's intoxicating and exciting to converse with God in this way, knowing the Eternal One invites us into a loving embrace.

How is God prompting you to respond as you connect to your passage? Offer to give God your thoughts and reflections, and invite God to use the Scripture to change you.

The fourth stage is *contemplatio.* Now is the time to slow your breathing, sit still, and rest in the presence of God. Free yourself from your own thoughts, let go of your own words and open your mind, heart, and soul to hear God speak. Enjoy the awe-inspiring experience of being in the presence of God. Do you sense that warm embrace around you? Do you see God's tears and touch God's pain? Are you grateful for God's loving presence? Offer appropriate prayers to God. Enjoy what God is doing and saying to you. Sit and think about a response. Is there a prayer or a song bubbling up inside you? Are you prompted to journal or create an image? Allow God's presence to flow uninhibited through you.

Practicing lectio divina encouraged me to listen more attentively not just to Scripture but also to my life and to the world I live in. It empowered me to get out into nature and walk around my neighborhood with a different perspective, truly looking, listening, tasting, touching, and smelling in a way I had not done before. It opened my eyes to the wonder of all God's creation.

There are many ways that this kind of reflective approach opens us to the awe and wonder of God's world. All we need to do is get out, walk, and take notice.

We all know that walking benefits our physical health. Like many of us, I have been caught up in the passion for Fitbit steps. Evidently, ten thousand steps a day reduces the risk of heart disease, colon cancer, and stroke; lowers blood pressure; controls weight; increases bone density; and helps prevent osteoporosis and much more.

Walking is great for our spiritual well-being too. It is the fastest pace for noticing something enough to truly see it and appreciate it fully, not just with our eyes but with all our senses in the way that children do. Not walking as in stair climbing but walking as in getting out to explore our neighborhoods with the intent to observe, learn, and interact. Walking is not meant to be done fast or alone. It is a form of noticing that is best done in company with others.

God's created world is my favorite place for walking. It is the ultimate arena of awe, inspiring all of us to think, question, form new ideas, and become creative. We can draw in the dirt like Jesus did, examine the wildflowers as he encouraged his followers to do, make designs with leaves, build forts with blankets, or just lie on the ground and admire the clouds. Nature is ever changing and inspirational. There is always something new to explore, create, and get excited about.

Tom and I now call our daily lakeside walks awe-and-wonder walks. We deliberately notice and point out to each other the inspiring sights of early morning light reflected in the lake, birds hovering in the sky and leaves slowly changing with the seasons. Walking our dog, we notice our neighborhood with the same awe. This garden is well kept with beautiful flowers in every season. That one is drab and neglected. We greet our neighbors and share stories about gardens and pets.

If we wander around the city, we notice and point out the urban lots transformed into community garden plots, the new skyscrapers rising into the sky, and the homeless people asleep in the doorways. We are enticed by the smell of coffee and baked goods from the cafe on the corner and enjoy the delight of making new friends. It is fun, and as we walk we often sense an awe-and-wonder song well up within us. Passigiata

It's a little like the disciples on the Emmaus road. They walked and talked. They were excited by the rumors of Jesus' resurrection. Awe and wonder bubbled up within them. Suddenly Jesus was walking with them (Luke 24:14-15). The exhilaration of sharing as we do when we walk and talk with others often brings Jesus into our midst explaining the Scriptures and how they reveal who he is. I wonder if that was the case for the disciples on the Emmaus road.

One beautiful walking practice created by St. John Providence Health System parish nursing in Michigan is "A Walk to Jerusalem" and "A Walk to Bethlehem." The idea is to improve the physical, emotional, and spiritual health of participants by taking imaginary trips to Jerusalem before Easter or to Bethlehem before Christmas.[8] Participants log their walking miles each week. Hopefully, by the time Easter arrives the total miles walked by all members of a church group will equal the number of miles to Jerusalem. Devotionals, prayers, and cultural information on the countries passed through provide wonderful resources to make this a fun and inspirational spiritual practice. These resources don't just talk about culture but also address societal needs participants would encounter if they actually walked to Jerusalem. For example, when they walk through the waters of the Atlantic, reflections focus on water scarcity, pollution, and sanitation.

> HOW WOULD IT CHANGE YOUR LIFE AND FAITH IF YOU TOOK REGULAR AWE-AND-WONDER WALKS?

Walking is for noticing not just sights, sounds, and smells but God, neighbors, and friends. How would it change your life and faith if you took regular awe-and-wonder walks? Why not try it? Go out and have a good walk today, notice your neighborhood, enjoy its sounds and smells and sights. Anchor yourself and find where you belong. Refresh your spirit and your soul. Come home and journal about what you experienced.

A NEW WAY OF SEEING

Walking a dog or admiring other people's gardens may not appeal to you, but there are other ways your noticing skills can enrich your spiritual life and open you to the awe and wonder of God's world. *Visio divina* or praying with art is becoming increasingly popular, not surprising in a world as visually oriented as ours. Orthodox Christians have long used icons to pray, but it is only recently that visio divina has become popular among Protestants. Religious art, street murals, photographs, and even graffiti can all provide inspiration for this practice.

Visio divina is similar to lectio divina but relies on images rather than words. It invites us to fully enter into an image, to take time to see deeply beyond first and second impressions. It inspires us to be transformed by new interpretations that God speaks through.

Choose an image, and take a slow look at it. Drink in the figures, colors, textures, and shapes. What draws your attention? Sit with your initial thoughts and feelings for a few minutes. Return to the image several times with an open heart and mind. Something new is likely to draw your attention each time. New thoughts, meanings, and feelings will arise. Your initial impressions should expand and deepen, allowing you to explore the image in fresh ways.

Prayerfully ponder your responses. What do you think the Spirit might want to reveal as you look and listen in quiet meditation to the feelings, thoughts, desires, and meanings evoked? Finish with prayer, taking time to respond to God with gratitude, supplication, wonder, lament, song, dance, or praise. Jot down responses in your journal as a reminder of the God-inspired awe the image awakened. Close by resting in God's grace and love.

The Book of Kells, an ancient illustrated Gospels manuscript with powerful images of saints and animals and beautiful calligraphy done by Celtic monks probably in the ninth century, is my favorite go to resource for visio divina.[9] The more recent St. John's Bible, a handwritten, hand-illuminated Bible created by renowned calligrapher Donald Jackson, also provides wonderful illustrations to contemplate.[10] Alternatively, you might like to visit your local art gallery and sit in front of a painting that catches your attention. Or use an image of your favorite painting or neighborhood street art.

A couple of years ago Tom and I had the privilege of walking around San Francisco with author and speaker Mark Scandrette. San

Francisco is one of our favorite cities. Tom spent much of his childhood there, and it is always a delight to return and walk the streets.

This time, however, Mark gave us a new visio divina way to view those streets, which inspired me with awe and wonder in places I had never imagined. He walked us through Balmy Alley, where murals first appeared in the mid-1980s in response to human rights and political abuses in Central America.[11] The murals grew to include human rights violations, gentrification, and Hurricane Katrina. We walked past life-size images of weeping women, rioting crowds, and massacred resisters. Among them, Christ dying in agony on the cross seared the images of pain, suffering, and liberation into my brain. I was stunned, awed, and humbled by people who endured so much. I was challenged to do something to prevent similar injustices in the future. This is one of Mark's favorite places to walk and reflect. I understand why.

For some, the new way of seeing is through the lens of a camera. Photography has blossomed as an art over the last few years. Everyone is taking and sharing pictures. Evidently, over four thousand are taken every second in the United States alone.

The moment we give close attention to anything, as the lens of a camera invites us to do, even a leaf dancing in the wind or an insect hovering over a flower can become awe inspiring, reminding us that we live in a world of wonder and mystery.

I have always loved photography, but it was Christine Valters Paintner who helped me interpret this joy as a special awe-inspiring encounter with God.

Look through the lens and imagine that it is a portal to a new way of seeing. Let the focus of the frame bring your gaze to the quality of light in this moment or the vibrancy of colors. Like in the film *American Beauty*, let yourself be willing to see the world differently, so that what others see as garbage becomes transfigured through your openness and intention. This isn't always easy, and ultimately it is God's work in us; we just create the right conditions to receive the gift.[12]

Not only has the lens become a portal to a new way of seeing for me, but my view of all images has gained the same holy revelation, bringing me an incredible amount of joy and a reawakening of awe in the process. I often stop to take a second look at everything from street signs to cracks in the road. Sometimes I do click a photo for future meditation. Sometimes I just pause for a moment of awe and wonder.

PRACTICE

Ten Miracles Before Breakfast

"Sometimes I've believed as many as six impossible things before breakfast," says Alice in Lewis Carroll's classic *Alice in Wonderland*. Awe and wonder make it possible for us to believe seemingly impossible things, as Alice did. So let's get out and give ourselves a good dose of awe and wonder this week.

Grab your camera, journal, and some pencils or colored crayons. Rediscover the miracles of life that surround you.

Get out into nature. Go for a walk in your favorite park or forest, or a picnic at your favorite beach, fully prepared to savor the experience with all your senses—listening, looking, tasting, touching, and smelling what you encounter. Look around at the trees and their leaves. How many different shapes and colors do you see?

See the world differently. Look through the lens of your camera or phone. What new perspective does this bring to the scene?

Take notice of the small things. Pick up an unusually shaped rock or shell. What attracted you to this object? What does it remind you of? Hold it in your hand. Touch it against your skin. How does it feel? How is it different from other objects around you?

Slow down and notice. Now find a quiet place to sit and contemplate your treasure. Use your crayons and permanent markers to create a pattern on it. Perhaps there are already patterns in the object that you can highlight. What comes to you as you paint? What does this small piece of creation tell you about God?

Seek out what gives you goose bumps. Now that your sense of awe has been stimulated, reflect back over your day. What else triggered a sense of awe in you? Was it an unexpected smile, a shared story, waves glistening on the sand? Try to make a list of at least ten "miracles" of awe and wonder that you experienced. How could you nurture more regular awareness of miracles like these?

Make space for silence. Sit quietly and take some deep breaths in and out. Close your eyes and remind yourself of the sights, sounds, fragrances, tastes, and textures of your day. Listen to God's presence in the day and contemplate what God's Spirit might say to you. Is there a prayer, song, drawing, or other response that comes to mind?

HAVE SOME FUN WITH FRIENDS

Recruit your spouse, your child, or a friend to explore with you. Plan a trip to your favorite park or beach together.

As you walk, marvel at your companion's perceptions and how differently they view the landscape. What excites them that you did not notice?

Allow time for each person to complete the previous reflective exercise on their own.

Sit around with a picnic lunch. Talk about the awe-and-wonder moments each person experienced.

Examine the objects they picked up and decorated. What attracted them to these objects? What added meaning did they give them? How did these inspire awe and wonder?

Read through the prayers, songs, and poems people added. Share the other responses that arose. Discuss your reactions.

LET YOUR LIFE SPEAK

Let God's love speak to you,
of the wonder of who you are,
the beauty of who
you are created to be.
Let God's love speak to you
of loyalty and generosity
and compassion,
of tenderness and caring and trust.
Let God's love speak to you
of fun and food and fellowship,
and what it means
to be a child of the living God.
Let it remind you that
God's love is so wide and deep,
so all embracing
that nothing can separate us from it.

There is nothing quite like a story to grab kids' attentions and fire their imaginations. They love to both listen to and tell them. When that story is about their own life and our memories of their birth and childhood they are riveted. They will listen to these stories over and over again.

It is not just kids who get excited when we reminisce. We all love to share our stories and know that they matter.

I discovered this when I stole an exercise from Tom that I now use in all my seminars. I get students to draw a picture of their life journey. They highlight when they felt close to God and when they felt distant. Everyone loves to share their stories and hear about the events and practices that shaped and strengthened their colleagues' faith. Like kids, everyone gets animated, joy filled, and hopeful.

In reminiscing, we awaken the fullness of our story and the awe and wonder hidden in it. The more we recount it, the more fully we understand and learn from it.

In *Brain Rules for Aging Well*, molecular biologist John Medina documents the surprising research that shows how important reminiscing and nostalgia are for our bodies. "Nostalgia promotes something called self-continuity linking who we were in the past with who we are now."[1] Reminiscing increases our social connectedness and sense of fulfillment in our accomplishments as positive memories rise to the surface. When we immerse ourselves in memories of our younger selves, we become healthy, our aches and pains are reduced, our weight and posture improve, and our dexterity increases. Even our eyesight gets better. According to researchers, "The key turns out to be multi-sensory immersion."[2] It makes me wonder what it does for our spiritual health too.

The first time I drew my own life story was an unexpected revelation. I drew my parents and three brothers but not myself. As a child, I often felt isolated from my family. As a premature infant I spent the first month of my life in hospital, alone and, from my infant perception, unloved. That obviously shaped my childhood and even adulthood.

I pulled out some photos from my childhood and ran my fingers over my mother's face as she held me in her arms. I smiled at my brothers and me dancing for glee on the beach and laughed at my early attempts at ballet. I am a loved and cherished child. In that moment of revelation, a deep peace from God flooded my heart and soul. *You were never alone,* I felt God say to me, *I was always with you.* A prayer welled up within:

> God, why did you abandon me,
> a tiny infant born before my time?
> Alone and afraid, caught in a web of machines,
> deprived of a mother's love,
> did you leave me with no one to care?
> No! You brought me out of the womb.
> Your love whispered in my mind.
> Soothing, comforting, embracing.
> You taught me to trust in you and held me in your arms.
> O Lord, you were never far off.
> You are my strength and my refuge, my salvation,
> you will never leave me.[3]

In retelling my story with God at the center, I found healing not just for that lonely infant part of my soul but also for my relationships with my parents and brothers. Pause and think about your own life. *What childhood stories might God want to remind you of? How could you reinterpret them with God at the center?*

ugh!

WHAT CHILDHOOD STORIES MIGHT GOD WANT TO REMIND YOU OF? HOW COULD YOU REINTERPRET THEM WITH GOD AT THE CENTER?

Telling our stories is powerful, even when there are pain and trauma we are not sure we want to revisit and it is far more than the nostalgia effect. Reminiscing often unveils the invisible hand of a loving God who shaped and guided us to become the people we are. When we neglect these stories, they hold us prisoner to fear and pain. Retelling them is an invitation to the exhilarating adventure of an awakened and full life.

Working on this chapter made me realize I needed to revisit my story. I have never retold it specifically asking, *What has God enjoyed about me and my life decisions?* As I sat in my quiet space thinking about this, "The kingdom of God is within you" (Luke 17:21 KJV), came to mind, "and within my story," I spontaneously added. Each step of my journey has given me glimpses of our awe-inspiring God and of God's new shalom world of wholeness and peace.

What did God enjoy about my birth, I wondered? God delighted over me from the moment of my conception I realized. God held me tenderly as I was taken to the neonatal care facility and placed in an infant incubator. God wept with joy with my mother who had finally given birth to a daughter after three sons. Every birth is a miracle, and God's heart fills with joy at the beauty, complexity, and uniqueness in me.

What did God enjoy about my childhood? In some ways that is harder for me to contemplate. My father's violent temper and angry explosions color my memories as did my perceived infant abandonment. Yet there was so much to look back on with delight. The sweet smell of my mother's embrace fills my senses. The joyful memories of family celebrations, vacations, and fun-filled playtimes with my brothers sweep over me. My medical studies and love of learning were a joy that I know God shared. The memory of that afternoon under the eucalyptus trees when I gave my heart to God overwhelms me with God's delight.

Looking back over my adult years, *What did God enjoy about me?* is a delightful remembering of my often hesitant steps into a closer relationship with God. My mind immediately focuses on my days on the mercy ship MV *Anastasis*. When I wrote my first book, *Tales of a Seasick Doctor*, I spent many evenings reminiscing with friends about this often crazy adventure. We laughed at the memories of fingers scraped raw as we literally built a hospital from scratch. We cried at the memories of deforming cleft lips and recounted the joy of palate repairs and cataract surgeries that transformed people who thought they would always live in the shadows. We wrinkled our noses as we were transported back to the refugee camps where the oppressive heat, mixed with smells of poor sanitation and chlorine, still overwhelm our senses. One morning after one of these sessions, a colleague asked me, "What on earth did you do last night? Everyone came in high as a kite this morning." Our retelling of stories that highlighted the faithfulness of God in our past energized and inspired all of us.

yes!

The kingdom of God is within all of us and within our life stories. Remembering and sharing our journeys isn't just fun, it is transformational, especially when we connect them to God's story. Recounting our past doesn't just say what happened, it explains why our life is important and why we as individuals matter. It gives us insights into the practices that have shaped our lives and how they have strengthened and encouraged spiritual growth.

REMEMBER THE STORY OF GOD

It's no wonder God constantly encouraged the children of Israel to reminisce about their story. They are told to remember so much that we often gloss over—the pain of slavery in Egypt (Deuteronomy 5:15), the wonder of being a special people set apart by God (Deuteronomy 7:6), the importance of the laws God gave them. I love the passionate way this is described.

> Make the things I'm commanding you today part of who you are. Repeat them to your children. Talk about them when you're sitting together in your home and when you're walking together down the road. Make them the last thing you talk about before you go to bed and the first thing you talk about the next morning. *Do whatever it takes to remember them:* tie a reminder on your hand and bind a reminder on your forehead *where you'll see it all the time*, such as on the doorpost where you cross the threshold or on the *city* gate. (Deuteronomy 6:6-9)

Remember, remember, remember! The more we remember our stories with God at the center, the more we are able to become the people we are meant to be.

Jesus specialized in telling stories that changed how his followers interpreted their lives and interactions with their world. Perhaps some of these stories encouraged them to remember their own history from God's perspective and learn to trust once more in the God who promised never to abandon them.

Did they identify with the prodigal son who wasted his inheritance and ended up in poverty, just as I am sure they felt had happened to *what ?* their nation? Did they see the loving father who greeted this son with joy and celebration as their loving God waiting patiently to welcome *finite !* them home? Did the good Samaritan remind them that they were once foreigners and therefore commanded to love the foreigners in their midst (Deuteronomy 10:19)? With so many Old Testament admonitions to "remember," I can't help but think this must have been so.

Jesus' stories also often gave glimpses of the kingdom of God. "The kingdom of God is like . . ." was a common way for him to begin. His passion for the generous, sharing, caring God he called Father and for the restoration of all this God had created rings through his stories of lost coins, hidden treasure, and good Samaritans. Images of reconciliation, healing, and justice abound in stories of prodigal sons, pruning of vines, and unjust landowners.

Jesus created vivid images of what God's love for us and God's concern for injustice looked like, reminding the Jews that they were God's special people called to be caring and compassionate. Perhaps these stories had them asking, "What does the kingdom of God look like in my life?" Maybe this is what inspired the little boy to give away his lunch, believing that the God who rained manna from heaven and could find hidden treasure and lost coins could also multiply his meager offering to feed thousands.

Jesus' stories, as well as his miracles, transformed his followers' perceptions of life, faith, and God as they reinterpreted their history and imagined a new world of justice, peace, and abundance, which many of them then set out to create. These stories were tangible and transfixing, and Jesus seemed to have an endless supply of them. They encouraged people to think outside the boxes of their usual religious and cultural perceptions and empowered them to confront and challenge the accepted way of doing things.

"The kingdom of God is like . . ." is still a good starting point for a story, and as I reflect on my own life story I love to think back with that phrase in my mind. "The kingdom of God in my life is like . . ." has been an inspiring and joy-filled exercise for me. It has brought to mind afternoon tea with friends, sharing garden produce with neighbors, and the delight of a budding rose. So many little things give us glimpses of the kingdom, but we often miss these moments of delight because we are overwhelmed by the big images that our craving for world peace and harmonious living conjure.

I often ask students, "What would your neighborhood look like if the kingdom of God came in its fullness?" We read about God's shalom in Isaiah 65:18-25 and imagine a neighborhood in which injustice, poverty, disease, and enmity are abolished. Then we tell stories that visualize God's new world in concrete and exciting ways.

Students usually start with, "There would be a church on every corner." Then come the blank stares. So I rephrase my question, "What good things would you like to see happen in your neighborhood?" Suddenly the lights go on—jobs for the unemployed, parks, gardens, and community gardens instead of vacant lots; fresh paint on houses, health clinics, cleanup of toxic waste, children's theater, murals on walls, and much more—beauty, abundant provision, laughter, and song. This is the *shalom of God*. It is an inspiring way for people to connect Bible stories to their lives and communities. Some have even gone on to make their stories into reality.

Viewing movies through the same "the kingdom is like . . ." lens is also inspiring. *Babette's Feast* is one movie that has motivated many with its banquet feast and the Christlike Babette, who gives up everything to provide it. Stories like this are even more powerful when we put ourselves into them. A few years ago Tom, who loves to cook more than anything else, prepared a lavish French meal of pheasant, goat cheese, and spinach salad, gourmet vegetables, and luscious desserts paired with French wine. We watched *Babette's Feast* beforehand and discussed the movie while we ate. It was wonderful to see friends transform their images of God's kingdom into reality.

RESTORE AND TRANSFORM

Looking back on our lives and telling stories like this is a great way to distinguish two types of spiritual practices we all need to anchor us—those that restore and those that transform. Identifying these has liberated me to explore new possibilities for my spiritual life with excitement and joy.

I was first introduced to this concept by anthropologist Paul Hiebert, who talked about restorative and transformative rituals he observed in traditional cultures.[4] *What a wonderful way to categorize spiritual practices*, I thought, and adopted the concept as a framework for my own explorations.   *But it does!*

I don't believe everything should change. We need stability zones that anchor us firmly in what we believe and why we believe it. These are the restorative practices that provide the bedrock of our faith—daily prayer, weekly worship, celebrations like Easter and Christmas. Like water on a rock, they slowly polish the roughness away and carve deeper channels God's love can flow through. They anchor our faith, reaffirm our sense of meaning in life, and intentionally connect our daily activities to the life, death, and resurrection of Christ.

Daily time with God is important for me, but as I looked back over my faith journey to identify my anchoring restorative practices, it wasn't what came to mind. It was making my much-loved morning cup of tea. This is my unchanging anchor. I cannot imagine my devotional time without it held firmly in my hands. In fact, when I travel I carry a small electric kettle with me so I can still make tea first thing in the morning.

Everything else has changed over the years as my faith has grown, but that cup of tea remains constant. Sometimes I sit in my quiet space and pray. Or I light a candle or recite a breathing prayer to center myself in the presence of God. At other times I read a psalm or Gospel passage. Or I contemplate the beauty of God's creation outside my window. Holding my cup of tea grounds me in the assurance that God will meet with me today and every day, surrounding me with love, comfort, and security.

Tom sits in our living room facing the fireplace where a beautiful print of John Alden and Priscilla Mullins hangs, which he inherited from his grandparents. This painting is his restorative anchor. He even carries a photo of the scene with him to ground his prayers when he travels.

WHAT RESTORATIVE PRACTICES ANCHOR YOUR FAITH JOURNEY AND PROVIDE STABILITY FOR YOU?

Looking back over your faith journey, what restorative practices have anchored your life and faith, providing stability for you?

Unfortunately, our restorative practices can become rigid and inflexible, draining rather than joy filling. During one life transition, I remember forcing myself to sit and read my Bible each morning. Then I realized I didn't need to, and it was as though a weight had lifted off my shoulders. God had something new in mind for me and was just asking me to take the time to listen.

Life isn't static, and our practices shouldn't be either. They eventually lose their meaning and enriching power. Transformative practices reshape and revitalize our faith, and restore our delight in God.

These are usually highly creative and cut across the accepted way of doing things.

Most cultures have transformative practices built into them—rites of passage from childhood to adulthood, graduation ceremonies, birthdays, harvest festivals, weddings, baby showers, and even funerals. These celebrations say, *change is happening; let's celebrate it*. Let's say goodbye to the old—often with joy but sometimes with grief—and embrace the new with anticipation and hopefulness.

Church is often the one constant, unchanging part of life. We get anxious and build walls rather than bridges to avoid the new that is emerging because we want to feel safe when we walk through the door and into the sanctuary. It is in fact just that—a sanctuary. Suggesting our spiritual practices need to change often feels like messing with the bedrock of our faith. That is exactly why we need transformative practices and why we need to distinguish between what shouldn't change and what can.

Jesus specialized in transformative practices that rebuilt his disciples' religious routines. From unusual approaches to prayer like spitting in the mud to trips through despised Samaria, where he added insult to injury by talking to a woman, he constantly cut across the accepted ways of doing things, creatively stirring his listeners to rethink their religious observances.

Meals with unlikely assortments of people also became transformative events that changed how the guests looked at people from different cultures and social strata. Water into wine at a wedding, eating with tax collectors and prostitutes, transforming a few fish and loaves into a banquet for many: these are wonderful, vivid images of Jesus' creativity and imaginative approaches that broke down barriers across social divides and made his followers hunger for the bread of heaven. These spiritual practices connected people to a God of joy and delight whose presence they craved as never before.

GO ON RETREAT

One important transformative practice Tom and I enjoy together that keeps our faith alive and exciting is a quarterly retreat that refocuses us and helps us set new goals for the future. These retreats get our lives back in sync with God's purposes.

We book into a local motel and get away from our usual routines. There is no definite structure, but they are always fun and always helpful, enabling us to grow and adapt our faith in response to changing circumstances.

I start by reading my last three months of journaling, reminiscing on my story from those months. Then I sit in silence, inviting the Holy Spirit to blow through my imagination with fresh energy and inspiration. "What did God enjoy about these months" has become the framework for my reflection. Sometimes I read a book or write poetry to inspire me. At other times I draw sketches, color pictures, or just sit and knit. These exercises all help reinforce my connectedness to God and prepare me for the changes my Creator wants to initiate in my life.

After a period of solitary reflection, Tom and I share together. Sometimes our thoughts run in sync and gain energy and insight from our common pathways. At other times we are in totally different places, but the questions we ask each other propel us forward. On one retreat after I shared that I needed a more contemplative approach toward life, Tom asked, "What does contemplation mean to you?" He helped change the trajectory of my future, encouraging me to begin the creative practices like prayer gardens and painting rocks that have become such an important part of my spiritual life.

Once the serious stuff is out of the way, we go out and celebrate. We have fun antiquing, sightseeing, or hiking. We go out for dinner. It is all part of our transformative practice, preparing us for the change that is coming whether we like it or not so that we aren't caught off-guard or destabilized by it.

There has to be a better Q than "What does God enjoy about...?"

On the second day we get down to serious business again. We set
goals for the next few months, not just for work and vocation but for
ugh !
our spiritual life, our marriage and community life, and even for relaxation and fun. It is so liberating to be able to relax into God's goals for
every area of life knowing that God rather than Tom and I are
in control.

*What transformative practices have helped you grow and reshape your
spiritual disciplines?*

In *The Cup of Our Life*, spiritual director Joyce Rupp reminds us that
wholeness does not come without change and growth. "The spiritual
life is both a journey
toward becoming whole,
and a journey about
change."[5] Change is one
of the few constants in

> WHAT TRANSFORMATIVE
> PRACTICES HAVE HELPED
> YOU GROW AND RESHAPE
> YOUR SPIRITUAL DISCIPLINES?

our world. We simultaneously love it and hate it. We dig in our heels
and resist because we are not sure how to cope with a world that will
be different. If we embrace the possibility of change and commit ourselves to become part of the change-making process, the experience
is transformative, and the new habits we find bring joy and provide
greater sanctuary and more safety than what we left behind. So reminisce, have some fun, celebrate your milestones. Look back with joy
and look forward with anticipation and hope.

PRACTICE
Listen to Your Life

Let's reminisce and reflect on what God enjoys about who we are and what we do.

Sit in your favorite chair and relax. Take some deep breaths in and out.

PS 139

Close your eyes and visualize the God who delighted to lovingly craft you in your mother's womb and nurture you as you stumbled through the first hesitant steps of childhood and grappled with the challenges of life. Picture God reaching down and rescuing you from your mistakes and brokenness because of that delight.

Remind yourself of how special and unique your journey is.

Pull out your journal.

Recount the story of your birth and the first year of your life. Pull out your baby photos and reminisce. Where are you aware of God in this beginning point in your life? What do you think God enjoyed about your birth?

Continue to reflect on those early days. What is your earliest memory of the love of God?

Where else do you sense God in your journey? Tell a story about the joy spots in your journey. Compose another that highlights the struggling points in your life.

Read prayerfully through these stories: What made you feel close to God and when did you feel distanced from God? What were the practices that sustained you and brought joy to your life?

Draw a picture. Find a big piece of paper and some colored pencils or pens. Draw a picture of your life journey as recounted in your stories. Draw a rough sketch in pencil first and then use colored pencils or pens to highlight the joy spots. Then color the struggling points. Allow your memories and the stirrings of your heart to choose the colors for you.

too vague!!

Enter the joy of God. Prayerfully reflect on your picture. Dialogue with the image. Where do you sense God's joy in your journey and the person you have become?

What restorative practices enhance your awareness of God's enjoyment? How could you nurture and strengthen these?

What transformative practices enabled you to grow and draw closer to God?

Respond to your impressions in writing, poetry, painting, music, or whatever form of creative expression you enjoy. *agen , too general*

HAVE SOME FUN WITH YOUR FRIENDS

Encourage participants to go through the preceding exercise before the meeting. Begin by sharing your stories in the group. Encourage people to bring childhood photos to share as part of this.

If you have time, draw a picture together of your common story. Here too you might like to share photos from the past. What fun things do you enjoy doing together? What do you do together that you think delights the heart of God? What are the restorative and transformative practices that bind your group together?

Enter into the delight God takes in you as a community and the joy God experiences when you share each other's joy.

There are hokey and vague activities. need simple, specific instructions you can follow easily to create something — then work with it to let it open insight + awareness.

UNLEASH YOUR INNER CHILD

Unleash your inner child.
Let laughter fill your days
and joy bubble up within you.
Let it ripple out around you,
with smiles and happy faces.
Release your inner self
of creativity and imagination.
Have fun, be free,
and remember Jesus tells us
that unless we change
and become like little children
we will never enter the kingdom of God.

Tom and I live in an intergenerational community called the Mustard Seed House, a 1910 house divided into three apartments. We inhabit the middle floor with a young family above us and several singles below. My office looks out over the backyard. I love to watch as the kids play on the swings, make mud pies in the garden, and creatively shape discarded boxes into play houses. Their laughter and songs of joy bubble up and ripple out toward me bringing a smile to my face and a lightness to my spirit. I often wish I could go out and join the fun.

On one occasion, five-year-old Catie "forced" us to join the fun. She made us all into chocolate tasters.

She excitedly handed out small pieces of chocolate to savor. We closed our eyes and sat with the chocolate on the palms of our hands, breathing in its rich aroma. We tasted it, noticing its texture, savoring the sweetness on our tongues and relishing the way it stirred all our senses, transporting us into a moment of pure bliss. With much laughter and hilarity we shared our thoughts. Then we opened our eyes and with great delight licked the now molten chocolate off our fingers. We became kids together. It liberated us and freed us to plan, create and innovate for the future of our community in a joyful and fun-loving spirit.

Watching kids play is beautiful. Being invited to join them is even more delightful.

I imagine this happened to Jesus wherever he went. When I worked in African villages, where the culture bore many similarities to the one Jesus lived in, swarms of kids always crowded around us. They laughed and played and tried to get us to join them just like Catie did. They got excited when we set up our clinics and treated their friends. They believed in us and welcomed us with great enthusiasm. I imagine kids danced and laughed and played around Jesus like this too. I am sure he relished their presence and was infected with their enthusiasm.

I experienced this same playful enthusiasm when we painted rocks one Easter Sunday. Our small community celebrated with a special meal, and we wanted something fun but not too religious to do as part of our celebration.

I hunted the garden for small, smooth stones that washed up perfectly for the task. I pulled out my paint pens and watched people get to work, hesitantly at first but with growing enthusiasm and creativity as the evening progressed. Colorful designs and words of prayer soon emerged. Laughter erupted, and in the midst we talked about faith, hope, and resurrection. I thought it would take half an hour, but two and a half hours later we had to throw everyone out. We were all having so much fun enjoying both each other and God that we didn't want to stop.

?! We don't usually think about having fun with our spiritual practices. For most of us, prayer and Bible study are very serious, intellectual, and often rather staid activities that stimulate our minds but don't always stir our hearts. Yet as I watch people come alive with renewed intimacy with God as they participate in fun-filled God focused exercises I find myself wondering if we need to rethink what spiritual practices are and how they connect us to God.

Painting rocks, coloring pictures, doodling, and other creative exercises that stir our imaginations and tap into our creativity are becoming important spiritual practices for many followers of Jesus. You can even buy journaling Bibles now with room to create and doodle in the margins. These kinds of practices have become an important part of my

> **WHAT CREATIVE AND PLAYFUL ACTIVITIES DO YOU ENJOY THAT COULD BECOME FUN SPIRITUAL PRACTICES FOR YOU?**

own spirituality and the workshops I facilitate too. They free our eyes and our hearts to embrace the invisible and mysterious God who waits for our praise.

What creative and playful activities do you enjoy that could become fun spiritual practices for you?

LIGHT UP YOUR BRAIN

Nothing lights up the brain like play, according to Stuart Brown, a psychiatrist, clinical researcher, and founder of the National Institute for Play, who studies the effects of play on people and animals. He believes play is as important as oxygen for our well-being and that it's a powerful force in nature that helps determine the likelihood of the very survival of the human race.[1] Adult play buffers us against the burnout of the hustle and bustle of busyness.[2] And from my perspective, anything that lights up the brain to that extent must be important to God.

According to Plato, "You can discover more about a person in an hour of play than in a year of conversation."

Play may be God's greatest gift to mankind. It's how we form friendships, and learn skills, and master difficult things that help us survive. Play is a release valve for stress, and an outlet for creativity. Play brings us music, comedy, dance, and everything we value.

Above all, play is how we bond with each other—it's how we communicate "I am safe to be around, I am not a threat."[3]

When we play well together, enemies become friends, we replace negative beliefs and behaviors with positive thoughts and actions and heal emotional wounds. It is, I suspect, meant to be an important part of our spiritual practices too.

Kids don't just have fun playing, they enter wholeheartedly into it, enjoying life in ways that adults rarely do. They dance, they sing, they get dirty. They forget about time and schedules. They ask questions but don't always wait for answers. So much that we could learn. We all need to play, make a mess, and get dirty, its part of how God created us. We need to learn once more to enter wholeheartedly into the en- *engage* joyment of life without allowing the cares and concerns of our world *Her* to overwhelm us. *Theology*

One consequence of sin is that work became toil and hardship. Play was pushed to the margins. For many, spiritual practices became toil and hard work too, with little fun and no laughter. This is, I suspect, part of the reason so many disconnect from church and lose interest in religious observances. Restoring the joy of play restores the joy of spiritual practice. It is part of our journey toward redemption and salvation.

Watching kids play, and relearning the art of embracing playfulness into our spiritual practices, unveils glimpses into the heart of our

play - spontaneity - now

fun-loving, playful God and into the joy-filled personalities God wants us to grow into. Play bonds us to God just as it does to each other and probably buffers us from the spiritual burnout so rampant in our faith communities. It liberates us to be ourselves and invites us to relax, take notice, and be unafraid to be vulnerable. I am convinced it is an essential but neglected element for the survival of our relationship to God.

Stuart Brown suggests that we need three types of play:

- *Body play:* participating in active movement with no time pressures or expected outcome

- *Object play:* using our hands to create something we enjoy with no specific goal in mind

- *Social play:* joining other people in seemingly purposeless social activities from small talk to verbal jousting[4]

As well as that, in *Play: How It Shapes the Brain* he identifies eight play personalities that help us determine what we are most likely to call fun.

- *The joker* is the class clown or prankster who loves to make others laugh.

- *The kinesthetes* are the movers and shakers who love to dance, run, walk, and swim. They need to move to think.

- *The explorer* loves to go new places, discover new ideas, meet new people, or search for new responses to music, art, or a story.

- *The competitor* doesn't just like to play games, they like to win. Keeping attention on the fun and not the winning may be a challenge for them.

- *The director* loves to organize, plan, and execute events. Planning a party or a family celebration, directing a play, creating a home movie, or getting friends together into a music band all appeal to this play type.

- *The collector* likes to gather experiences, objects, or people. Some go places just to be able to add them to their collection.

- *The artist/creator* finds joy in making things—anything from arts and crafts to gardens, buildings, and toys.

- *The storyteller* is the imaginative type who loves to write stories, draw cartoons, read, or watch movies. They tell stories to imaginary friends, illustrate stories others tell with pictures, and love to relate Bible stories in their own expressive ways.[5]

Understanding my play personality gave me permission to play again and incorporate playful practices into my spirituality. It has lightened my spirit and brought me joy. I often knit or paint rocks while I pray or make messy doodles in my journal. It's such fun. What form of play delights us does not really matter; most of us combine play personalities. What is important is that we continue to delight in play.

What play personality do you most identify with?

When I thought about this for myself, I realized that many playful activities still light up my brain, and over the last few years I have channeled some of these passions into my spiritual life. My earliest memory of play is building with my brother's erector set. I also loved exploring new places, and my parents often planned circuitous routes so that my discovery of our homeward journey was delayed as long as possible. Exploring and creating still light up my brain and have led to pilgrimages and explorations of churches, art galleries, and new cities.

As I grew older, collecting—rocks, feathers, and plants—became more of a playful passion for me. As an adult, I have redirected this energy by collecting and painting rocks and creating gardens as tools for reflection.

I am a born organizer too. Facilitating events is fun for me. My brothers and friends suffered through many cycling and hiking trips I planned. They still enjoy my parties, vacations, and outings. Organizing not only gives me joy but also inspires my creativity and connectedness to God. However, it can become a burden if I overbook myself. Recognizing it as play rather than work and seeing this as a way to bring pleasure to God has made it enjoyable once more.

What is your earliest memory of play? Is it with a toy, at a birthday party, on a vacation, at the zoo? What emotions did it evoke? How does this connect to your life now, and how could you incorporate this type of play experience into your life so that it adds joy?

What playful experiences bubble up from your childhood memories that God is prompting you to reimagine as spiritual practices?

For Angie Fadel it was archery that bubbled up from within.[6] One of her earliest childhood memories is of wanting to learn to shoot a bow. Her dad made her first bow from sticks and string on a camping trip when she was five or six. She asked over and over for every cartoon, movie, book, or image, male or female, depicting an archer. These ideas followed her into childhood, and then when her husband and a friend gave her archery for her birthday, she was hooked.[7] Now Angie, a spiritual director in Portland, Oregon, conducts workshops on meditative archery to help people get in touch with their tough emotions like rage, anger, and fear. Her passion, planted in childhood and grown throughout her life, has become a spiritual practice that has strengthened both her life and those of many others.

> WHAT PLAYFUL EXPERIENCES BUBBLE UP FROM YOUR CHILDHOOD MEMORIES THAT GOD IS PROMPTING YOU TO REIMAGINE AS SPIRITUAL PRACTICES?

PLAY PRAYERFULLY

Reading about the power of play to light up our brains meant I wanted this for my spiritual practices too. My first experiments were not particularly successful, partly because I did not take the time to think about how I like to play. I was given a couple of beautiful Scripture-focused coloring books and tried to pray while I colored. I hated it. The intricacy of the designs and my compulsion to color until finished left me tense and frustrated rather than relaxed and joyful.

Then I started playing with my collection of rocks and shells, arranging them in circles, question marks, and heart shapes. I glued them to sketch paper and wrote around them. It was fun and created meaningful focal points for my meditations. Next, I purchased a set of paint pens and wrote words and inspiring phrases on my rocks. They were pretty messy but helped center my prayers and thoughts. I added my love of gardening into the mix and soon put together my first prayer garden. I loved it and am sure my brain lit up with delight.

Play is increasingly at the center of my creative-spirituality workshops too. I provide coloring sheets, pencils, and pens and encourage participants to use these throughout the event. I allocate time for drawing, painting, and writing prayers. At times it is a little scary as people relax, open up, and share stories of battles with cancer, abuse, or addiction as well as their doubts about God. Playful activities allow them to be themselves and share their vulnerability. All I need to do is give them permission to be themselves and then listen.

When my experimenting with rock painting as a form of prayer was in its infancy, I had the incredible privilege of teaching a course on spiritual renewal for a group of church leaders from Myanmar, the Philippines, South Korea, Vietnam, Jamaica, Kenya, Ghana, and Uganda. The group was not only ethnically diverse but also denominationally—everything from a Catholic nun to a Pentecostal preacher. Finding practices that appealed to everyone was not easy, but when I suggested we do some rock painting they came alive. I sent students out to gather rocks with strict instructions not to disturb anyone's garden, but some of them returned with huge stones that I couldn't imagine they had just found along the wayside. Beautiful works of art emerged with crosses, prayers, and colorful designs that spoke of their life experiences and their hopes for the future. Many students planned to take them home in their hand luggage.

Ruth, a nun in her eighties, recently took up whittling as a hobby. She now whittles while she prays, a practice that is not only enjoyable for her but has greatly enriched her relationship with God too.

Play therapy has become an increasingly important practice for encouraging children to explore life events and the effect of trauma on their behavior. It can help individuals communicate, explore repressed thoughts and emotions, and experience personal growth. My experience as well as Sister Ruth's show that it is just as important for spiritual growth too.

Godly Play is an impressive curriculum for children that recognizes the power of play. It came out of the creative inspiration of theologian, author, and educator Jerome Berryman and helps children explore their faith through story, wonder, and play, and helps them encounter the mystery of God's presence in their lives. "It engages what is most exciting about religious education: God inviting us into, and pursuing us in the midst of, Scripture and spiritual experience."[8]

Godly Play offers an alternative approach to religious education. Each session begins with the children gathering in a circle around the material that will tell their story for the day. There might be figures set up to depict biblical scenes, candles or other religious objects, photos, toys, and more. The storyteller unfolds the story using the objects in the circle, taking plenty of time to focus on the material. Then, the storyteller asks "wondering" questions that help slow down the teaching pace while not slowing down the learning process. "I wonder which is your favorite part of the story?" "I wonder which is the most important part?" "I wonder where you see yourself in the story." "I wonder where the story is about you."

Next, children explore their ideas through creative responses. They leave the circle and grab some paints; clay; construction materials like Lego blocks, collage materials, or a notebook for poetry; or a musical instrument. The session ends with a meaningful sharing of children's ideas and a sending-out prayer.[9]

Godly Play teaches us to listen for God and make authentic and creative responses to God's call in our lives. "Because spirituality and Christian language acquisition are lifelong journeys, use of the *Godly Play* method has quickly grown to include adults, the elderly and children in a diverse variety of setting such as hospitals, residential care facilities, prisons and by facilitators of social justice."[10]

Deacon Lois Howard, in the Episcopal diocese of Lexington, Kentucky, introduced the *Godly Play* program to people suffering from Alzheimer's disease. She says: "It is not unusual for us to talk briefly after the weekly story and hear memories tumble out, memories of their childhood. There is something about the way in which these stories, using the three dimensional figures, seem to trigger the memories of the people hearing them."[11]

DON'T BE AFRAID OF A LITTLE MESS

My growing use of play-oriented spiritual practices sent me looking for fun-filled faith-shaped observances that others have created too. Biblically-based celebrations are my favorites. *ugh!*

Our own church, St. Andrew's Episcopal in Seattle, adapted the Jewish Seder meal into a beautiful Agape feast for Maundy Thursday. We join Jesus and the disciples in that final Passover meal and then begin the walk with him toward the cross. We eat roast lamb and rice pilaf. We share horseradish and bitter herbs, eaten by the Hebrews on Passover because they were slaves in Egypt and their lives were bitter. We participate in a litany adapted from both the Jewish Seder and the Christian tradition. We laugh and have fun, and as we do so I imagine the disciples laughing and enjoying the feast with us.[12]

Then the mood turns more somber. We wash each others' feet as a reminder that Christ calls us to serve, not to be served, and end the evening with Communion before processing into the sanctuary to strip the altar. It is one of the most meaningful Holy Week services I have ever attended, and I know that the fun we share and the playfulness of our feasting is part of what provides such an indelible memory for me and for many others who participate.

Another practice I would love to try is the "Tongues of Fire Chili Cook-Off" of Faith Episcopal Church in Laguna Niguel, California, an annual Pentecost event.[13] It has turned into an entertaining community-wide event, with prizes based on spice level and flavor. Recipes are posted on the church website. While it's not part of the liturgy itself, it is a creative way to use symbols in the life of the community, and it can't help but transform a simple meal into a teachable moment.

Messy Church is a church movement that recognizes the importance of play. Children and adults meet together in creativity, storytelling, celebration, and hospitality. It's a little like Montessori at church, using hands-on activities to explore Bible stories, reflect the God of creativity, and give people a chance to play together. Messy Church leader Lucy Moore explains:

> Messiness means creativity, risk and humility in the way we approach other people and ideas. Messiness is content with loose ends, unresolved issues, development, spontaneity, fluidity and tensions, because family life is full of them and they are a vital part of how we become who we are meant to be together. It treats other people as potential rather than problem. It accepts that process is as important as product. . . . It is a place of power because it refuses to take hold of power. Messiness is a throwing-off of protective shoes to step vulnerably, with messy feet that need the washing of the only person who is qualified to do it, into the holy ground of loving God, loving our neighbour and loving ourselves. . . . We find the pearl of great price in messy places. Messiness is a holy mystery.[14]

Messiness is content with loose ends. Messiness is holy mystery. What beautiful thoughts to bring to our spiritual quest where doubts and unanswered questions often feel like loose ends that could unravel at any moment.

Most churches would not feel comfortable with the disorder of Messy Church, but there are elements of childlikeness we can all bring into our worship services that would increase our enjoyment of God and bring rejoicing to the heart of God.

For example, creative worship leader Lilly Lewin always takes her sketch book to church and doodles her way through the sermon. Other attendees often ask her if it is really okay to draw or color in church. When she says yes, it can be very liberating for them, a way to free up that creative childlike energy that is waiting to be expressed. They start to unleash the creativity God has placed within them, and in the process learn that church really can be fun.

When expressive arts therapist Kim Balke set up a "creation station" with clipboards, paper, and markers at the back of her church, it was initially used by children. Now a surprising number of adults have caught on and discovered how helpful doodling and drawing can be as listening and creating tools during worship. Some write down key words from the sermon and doodle around them as they reflect. Others just draw or doodle as background to the sermon. They too are rediscovering their God-given playful creativity and how powerfully it can help grow our faith.

Lilly and Kim inspired me not only to reimagine my personal spiritual practices but also to rethink the way I give sermons. I hand out decorative crosses and colored pencils and give people permission to be creative while I talk. I love walking around afterward looking at what people create. Some just color. Others write notes or doodle around the image. In the process they often learn something profound about themselves and the God they are learning to enjoy in new ways.

PRACTICE
Plan a Playdate

Plan a playdate with your children, grandchildren, or a friend's children. If the weather is good, go to the nearest playground and watch the kids play. Record their laughter, take photos of their play. Enter into the emotions of the children you are with (for example, their delight in swinging higher than their friends). What is your earliest memory of a playground visit? What emotions does that memory stir?

If it is raining, you may prefer an at-home playtime. Pull out some paints and paper or crayons and coloring books and let the kids get into some messy, creative play. Join in the fun. Dip your fingers in the paint and smear them on the paper. Or if you feel really adventurous, dip your whole hand in the paint and create handprint patterns.

Alternatively, pull on your rain boots and coats and go for a walk in the rain. Enjoy the feel of raindrops on your face. Put out your tongue and taste the drops. Smell the rich fragrance of ozone in the air. Splash in the puddles when the kids do. Jump in the mud and get dirty with them.

Notice what the kids notice. Laugh, play, dance, free yourself from the inhibitions of adulthood. Enjoy yourself.

Time to reflect. Take time afterward to reflect on the experience.

Sit prayerfully in a quiet place and think back over your playdate.

- How did it make you feel?

- What gave you the greatest joy?

- Journal about the day. You might even like to add the impression of your paint-smeared or mud-splattered hand to the book.

- What do you think God enjoyed about the day?

- How did this affect your understanding of God's delight in you?

Respond. Think about the creative impulses this day stirred within you. Draw a sketch, doodle, paint a picture, make it into a piece of art. You might be inspired to write a song or a poem. Or perhaps you want to plan an event or build something as a result.

In what ways does this make you feel closer to God and enhance your sense of God's delight in you? How could you incorporate it into your spiritual practices?

HAVE SOME FUN WITH FRIENDS

Plan a playdate with your small group and recruit their kids to go with you. Go to the local children's play area. Take a picnic lunch or dinner. Get on the swings with the kids. Allow yourself to be swept up into childlike delight at the motion of the swing, the joy of going higher than you have gone before, and the awe and wonder of sights and sounds you have never noticed before. Have some fun. Afterward, sit on the grass to eat your meal and reflect on the previous questions.

If it is raining, pull on your rain boots and coats and go for a walk in the rain. Enjoy the feel of raindrops on your face. Put out your tongue and taste the drops. Smell the rich fragrance of ozone in the air. Splash in the puddles when the kids do. Jump in the mud and get dirty with them.

Go home for a picnic-type meal together. What made you laugh and want to dance? Reflect on the previous questions together. Discuss how this made you feel closer to God and ways to incorporate your experience into your spiritual practices.

Play = dived experien

SET YOUR IMAGINATION FREE

God of creation come to us.
In the breaking light of dawn,
in the awesome beauty of life,
speak to us of your unfailing love.
God of creativity come to us.
In the imagination of thought,
in the diversity of form,
in the infinity of design,
show us the wonder of who you are.
May this day rise to meet us
with new horizons
that beckon toward fresh beginnings.
Let it awaken our spirits to adventures
that excite our hearts
and uncover undiscovered gifts.
May its rhythm
keep us in step with your eternal breath,
alive with glimpses of glory,
whispers of love,
splashes of joy.

I am something of a dreamer, a lover of science fiction novels, and a believer in the power of imagination to change the world. When

Harry Potter catapulted into the imagination of kids, I was right there with them, delighting in the creativity that brought this magical world into being.

I am particularly intrigued by authors who imagine worlds and technologies that don't exist and even more amazed by the artists and scientists who eventually make their ideas become reality. Jules Verne's vivid description of the Nautilus in *20,000 Leagues Under the Sea* made a lifelong impression on the young Simon Lake, who grew up to become the father of the modern submarine. Dick Tracy's two-way wrist radio and Star Trek's communicator inspired the creators of our cell phones.

Albert Einstein believed that imagination was more important than knowledge.[1] When we tap into our imaginations, we dream of what could be, open ourselves to different choices, and set in motion the creation of a new reality that can dramatically change both our future and our world's future. Imagination is transformational. It ignites passion, rekindles hope, and restores joy.

Kids are alive with this kind of imagination. They're always creating new things, new worlds, new possibilities. Give them a cardboard box, and they create a space ship. Give them a paintbrush and some paper, and landscapes that abound with purple clouds and blue trees soon appear. They tell fanciful stories of dragons and fairies, of magic and mystery. Ask them what they want to be when they grow up, and you may hear wonderful Peter Pan–type stories of adventure and fun. These stories sound fanciful to us, but they often express the deepest dreaming of a child's heart. They believe not necessarily in the existence of such worlds but in the meaning and values those worlds depict, and sometimes they go on to make these worlds a reality.

Unfortunately, our playful, imaginative selves often get buried in the adult world where we are encouraged to get a job, find a partner, become "responsible" citizens. Yet God's creative energy is still alive and well. Russian philosopher Nikolai Berdyaev said, "God created the world by imagination," and in Isaiah 48:6-7 we read,

> I am telling you new things,
> secrets hidden that no one has known.
> They are created now—brand new, never before announced,
> never before heard.

No wonder Celtic Christians believed imagination was the sacred arena in which the individual connected to our Creator. God still creates with the same imaginative energy that brought us and our world into being. Imagination and creativity are at the core of who God is and who God created us to be. Our job is to learn to take notice of what our imaginations are observing, processing, and expressing, just as kids do.

Sometimes imaginative inspiration comes from the traditional events of the church calendar. For example,

> On Ash Wednesday 2010, three Chicago-area Episcopal congregations independently took ashes and prayer to suburban train stations, and discovered commuters hungry for a moment of prayer, renewal and grace. Those who had no time to attend services or had forgotten about the tradition were delighted to receive ashes with prayer as they began their day. Many responded with tears or smiles of gratitude that the church would come to them.[2]

Now groups around the world participate in offering ashes to people where they are—on street corners, outside coffee shops, at bus and train stations. It brings joy and a moment of grace to people in the midst of daily life.

What stirs your imagination and gets your creative juices flowing? Sit and think about the imaginative activities you enjoy that you feel also bring joy to God. Dig back into your childhood memories. Is there a skill or area of interest you were passionate about but never had the opportunity to fully enjoy or develop? Perhaps your passion was lost as the "real world" of economic security, educational excellence, and family priorities took over. Maybe you were told "there is no money in it" and discouraged from pursuing your dreams. Reimagine this activity as an encounter with your imaginative, fun-loving Creator. Visualize yourself basking in the pleasure of God as you practice your skill. How does it alter your impression of it? Is there a creative response God is nudging you to make?

> WHAT STIRS YOUR IMAGINATION AND GETS YOUR CREATIVE JUICES FLOWING?

STIRRING OUR IMAGINATIONS

New Zealand worship curator Mark Pierson set my imagination free. Mark, who describes himself as an artist whose medium is worship, is one of the most creative people I know. He designs and plans corporate worship events that create sacred spaces in the most unlikely places.

Mark curated worship for a conference we facilitated ten years ago, and the power of it still affects me. He transformed an ordinary room into a beautiful sacred space using only a trellis-like fence with a basket of barbed wire "crosses" at its base and a parcel of zip ties.

Our beginning prayer acknowledged our gathering as being in Seattle, named after Chief Seattle of the Dwamish and Suquamish people, who are the traditional guardians of this place. We committed ourselves to care for the land with them and prayed that our service would work together for peace and reconciliation. Mark showed PowerPoint slides of refugees, at that time fleeing from Iraq and Afghanistan. He read Matthew 25:31-40 from *The Message* and then asked, "What's at the bottom of your heart when you think of refugees? What are the names of immigrants you know?"

Mark explained that zip ties are used as handcuffs in many parts of the world. Then he asked us to reflect on this and pray for refugees and illegal immigrants who are forcibly constrained with them. We brought the zip ties forward and attached them to the fence as a symbol of identification with the suffering of those struggling to settle into a new land as well as those detained falsely and unjustly. Finally, we took one of the barbed-wire "crosses" to remind us that Jesus has accepted each of us as we are and that we should accept others as generously. Mark suggested we carry the "cross" in our hand throughout the day.

Mark believes that corporate public worship events should be seen more as art forms through which people engage with God rather than teaching processes that convey information about God. There is no one-size-fits-all when it comes to designing events that enable people to engage with God with heart, soul, mind, and strength.[3]

Such sacred spaces do not need to be confined to buildings either. Following the 2010 Christchurch earthquake, Mark's friend Peter Majendie constructed a graphic memorial with 185 empty chairs on the site where the Oxford Terrace Baptist Church was destroyed. The chairs are many shapes and sizes, all painted white to symbolize those who lost their lives. The individuality of each chair pays tribute to the uniqueness of each person. This has now become a permanent memorial, a special sacred space for all who visit or even for those of us who observe from afar. Having lost a dear friend in the earthquake, I revisit my photo of the memorial periodically to pray. It has ministered to me profoundly.[4]

Worship curator Lilly Lewin is another person who helped set my imagination free. On a recent visit to Nashville, she took me to an extrasensory workshop at the Frist Museum. We were handed a clipboard with paper on it and an apron to wear so we wouldn't get covered in paint, and then we were directed to a collection of bottles infused with scents. We sniffed at everything from cedar and lavender to pipe tobacco and fireplace ash identifying what appealed to us.

I grabbed the lavender and cedar, and we moved on to a rich array of paints—every color of the rainbow. Dabs of red and violet and purple, light and dark green and brown and white, all the colors that resonated with my scents soon adorned my board. I sat down and pondered the memories that my scents stirred—my mother sweet with lavender perfume, heady lavender fragrance in my garden, aromatic cedar forests in the Pacific Northwest. I closed my eyes and contemplated my memories. Then I began to paint not with a brush but with a rag. I rubbed dabs of red and white and purple together allowing my imagination to blend the colors. Then I worked with the greens and brown and white again until a vivid and colorful image emerged.

It was fun, messy, and creative. I wanted to do it again and went home to plan my own process with my own creative twist.

What ignites our imaginations is as diverse as we are. Nature, art, music, painting, sculpture, woodwork, knitting, storytelling, and even arguing get our creative juices flowing. The more inspired we get, the more ripples of creative energy flow out through our lives.

When I asked my friend Kim Balke how to stir my imagination, she encouraged me to read children's books to foster a receptive posture of openness, wonder, and creativity. Afterward, she suggested I respond with a doodle, drawing, or poem. She even encouraged me to keep a few rhythmic instruments like a drum or singing bowl handy so that I could discover the sounds that resonated with what I read.

Her idea excited me. On a recent trip to Australia I had purchased a special book from my childhood called *The Magic Pudding*. Written and illustrated almost one hundred years ago by Norman Lindsay, an amazingly creative artist, sculptor, and writer, it is alive with wonderful, imaginative drawings of talking wombats, koalas, and kangaroos. To be honest I hardly looked at them until Kim unleashed my inner child in this way. After all, I am no longer a child. My adult self valued the memories rather than the story or pictures. Now I relish the innovative depiction of Australian animals. Their creation stirred the imaginations of many Australian kids and certainly stirred mine again as I reflected on them.

It was, however, *The Harmony Tree: A Story of Healing and Community*, written by Native American theologian Randy Woodley, that convinced me of how powerful this kind of storytelling is as a spiritual practice. This beautiful story, inspired by Randy's farm where virgin trees were logged years ago leaving one large white oak at the top of the hill, tells about Grandmother Oak, also spared when the forest is logged. When trees are replanted, she tries to befriend them but finds they are shallow and self-focused. Then she shares stories of how her own roots grew deep and strong, and as she does she finds healing for herself and strength for the new trees.

Reading this story, admiring the beautiful illustrations, and entering into the struggles and triumphs of Grandmother Oak wasn't just fun. I wanted to respond in ways that a list of facts about environmental degradation would never have motivated me to do.[5]

Another effective tool Kim taught me is doodling. This seemingly random and chaotic act that many of us engage in unconsciously unleashes our imaginations and draws us into a newly inspired relationship with God, especially when we do it with our nondominant hand.

I love to sit with a blank sheet of paper prayerfully asking God about how to enrich my spiritual practices. I hold my pen in my left hand, close my eyes and doodle for thirty seconds. I open my eyes and contemplate what I drew. Often a shape emerges that holds my attention. I play with it, grow it, and allow it to emerge in all its fullness. I add color and design and ask: *Where does this image come from? What does it need to be complete?* As I do, I sense God's joy in my image and, more profoundly, in my creative stirrings as I apply my insights to my spiritual life.

Doodling like this not only inspires our imaginations, it also builds trust. As we allow the creative process and the Creator of that process to take us where we need to go, amazing things happen.

In her book *Praying in Color*, Sybil MacBeth describes how she stumbled on a doodling form of prayer while relaxing on the porch with a basket of colored markers one afternoon.

> I opened a pad of Manila paper and started to draw. I doodled a random shape into existence with a thin black pen. Without even realizing it, I wrote a name in the center of the shape. The name belonged to one of the people on my prayer list. I stayed with the same shape and the name, adding detail and color to the drawing. Each dot, each line, and each stroke of color became another moment of time spent with the person in the center. The focus of the drawing was the person whose name stared at me from the paper. . . .
>
> To my surprise, I had not just doodled, I had prayed.[6]

I think her imaginative approach to prayer reconnected her to her inner child. It has done the same for her followers and has brought enrichment and delight to many of my friends. I am sure it delights the heart of God too.

Doodling opened my mind to imagine spiritual patterns in other unlikely places too. Like when I splattered wax from a candle all over my Lenten altar. It clung to my Palm Sunday cross, made splotches on my rock with "let love speak" written on it, and ran down the front of my purple tablecloth. It even landed on my fingers, painfully reminding me that wax is hot. Worst of all, it disturbed my altar's orderly arrangement, and I still haven't been able to get it off.

This happened as I reflected on the question, How do we use our freedom to serve others in love? The splattered wax provided revelation for me. The wax is like God's love, splattered everywhere, adhering in the most unlikely places, creating beauty in unexpected ways, giving birth to new patterns. That is what freedom is all about.

Love is the candle of God burning in our lives, and as it burns, the wax melts and runs over everything in its path. Random acts of kindness, a smile and unexpected greeting from a stranger, a meal shared with new neighbors: they are all like splattered wax. They adhere to our skin and our lives in unexpected ways. They can be painful because they make us vulnerable, but they free us from the order and rigidity of a life controlled by us rather than by God.

Sit and think for a few moments: Where has God splattered love unexpectedly that brought freedom to you and to others? What actions of yours have helped spread the love and create that freedom?

Scraping the wax off myself and my desk wasn't easy. It was messy. Love sticks. It doesn't want to be scraped off. Where has love adhered to you in ways that have pushed you out of your comfort zones and created messiness? What has been your response?

Our world abounds with images that suggest God loves doodling too—or maybe that is just my imagination at work. Look down from an airplane at a river meandering across the landscape in seemingly random patterns of loops and curls and it looks as though God is doodling here!

Nature is full of what we call fractal images, complex doodle-like patterns created by repeating a simple process over and over in a feedback loop. We see these patterns in trees and rivers, in clouds, and even weather patterns like hurricanes. They are sometimes called images of chaos, but I think they would be best described as divine doodles.

HOW OFTEN DO I CONFINE THE RIVER OF GOD AND BUILD IMPENETRABLE BARRIERS TO ITS FLOW BECAUSE I DON'T WANT GOD TO CHANGE MY COURSE?

Examining God's doodles with an imaginative mind is a joyful spiritual practice in itself. I watch the river flow around a boulder and think, *There are no obstacles in God's world, just opportunities to choose a new path.* I see it overflow its banks and deposit its life-giving nutrients on the soil, and I applaud that God loves to renew and refresh us with physical and spiritual food. We run into problems only when we confine the river with levees and dams because we don't want it to change direction. In that too I learn. *How often*, I wonder, *do I confine the river of God and try to build impenetrable barriers to its flow because I don't want God to change my course?*

LET'S HAVE AN ARGUMENT

Perhaps doodling and painting or reading stories don't appeal to you, but there are many ways to engage our imaginations that can enrich our faith and bring new meaning to Jesus' stories.

One way we rarely consider is arguing, not the shouting, abusive confrontations we so often see on the news, but reasoned disagreements, more like debate. Kids delight in this kind of discourse. They often enjoy disputing their parents just for the fun of it. To be honest I am rather fond of a good argument too.

Jewish theologians believe arguing is one of the highest forms of theological discourse. They feel dissenting voices are essential. When everyone in a gathering holds the same viewpoint, someone volunteers to be the dissenter. I can understand why. Grappling with diverse theological views reveals new and unexpected horizons. It can be a fun way to talk about God, faith, and our struggles.

I suspect that Jesus sometimes used the practice too. He and the stories he told reveal he didn't fit into the adult world he lived in. Like the children around us, his stories were often disruptive, bothersome, and unpredictable argumentative discourses that stirred conversation, made people think, and often changed their viewpoints.

Read a parable from a variety of theological perspectives. Look for an upside down viewpoint that challenges what you were taught. Let your family or friends interpret it with you. Argue with each other about the meaning. Write or draw what comes to mind. Imagine games and activities to go with the story.

One of my favorites to do this with is the parable of the talents. Our traditional interpretation, which applauds the wealthy landowner, flatters the rich and powerful, but theologian Ched Myer has an upside down interpretation that is good for us to read and grapple with.[7] He believes the third slave, the one who buries his talents, really portrays Jesus. He sees the landowner as taking advantage of the workers who make money for him; their "reward": they receive a new job with more responsibility. The slave who refuses to buy into the system is cast out.

Different? Provocative? Something for us to struggle with? Yes all of these, but still an interpretation that helps us stir our imaginations and grapple with new possibilities.

Once you have read these different interpretations, consider retelling the story with yourself as one of the main characters. Play the part of the rich landowner, then become the slave who multiplies his talents ten times. Finally, become the slave who buries his money. How does playing each of these roles affect you and your audience? What questions does it raise, and what discussions does it trigger? How does it affect your view of the storytelling Jesus and of your faith?

Read a Children's Book

When was the last time you looked through a children's book for your own enjoyment and inspiration? When was the last time your inner child emerged to teach you?

Find a copy of your favorite children's book. If you don't have one at home, borrow from the local library.

Sit in a quiet place, still your mind, and imagine you are five years old again and sitting on your mother's knee. Read through the story aloud; let it resonate in your soul. Examine the illustrations. Touch them, trace them with your finger as a child would. Watch for your inner response. Write down what you sense God saying to you.

Look through the book again. What thoughts stir as you read the story? What images come to mind as you look at the pictures? Is there a song hidden in your heart in response? Does an image to draw emerge in your mind?

What creativity does this exercise ignite within you, and how do you feel God is prompting you to respond? Perhaps you would like to rewrite the story in your own language or with yourself as the central figure. Write, draw, record, or create your response in whatever media you are inspired to use. Alternatively, if you have a drum, a singing bowl, or another rhythm instrument handy, pull that out and discover the sounds that are reminiscent of what stood out for you in the story.

Or grab a set of children's LEGOs and build something.

HAVE SOME FUN WITH FRIENDS

Bring a Bible translation like *The Message* or *The Voice* to your meeting.

Choose one of your favorite Bible stories and read the story aloud. Pass the book around. Get each person to read a page or two.

Discuss how you would reimagine this as a children's story.

What is the main idea this story communicates that you would like to share with children? What are some creative images you could use to do this?

Get each person to rewrite the story either in words, pictures, song, or other media and share their stories.

What did you learn from this exercise? Is there an idea that emerged that you would like to apply to your spiritual practices?

GIVE YOURSELF THE GIFT
OF CURIOSITY

The world dances in wild abandon
to the rhythms of God.
Let us listen with our ears
and look with our eyes
to its holy song.
It is so ordinary, so simple,
yet so powerful,
this seeking after God.
Every daily act,
every jagged rock and babbling brook,
every darkened alleyway
and fast-paced city street
cries out God's voice,
begging to be listened to,
to be watched, handled, and examined.
All is a gift from God.
Let us receive with wonder and awe.

Asking questions is part of the joy and inspiration of childhood.
Kids don't want a simple yes or no response either. Their curiosity
and thirst for knowledge have them asking why, what, and how on

everything from the number of grains of sand on the beach to why people die. They have no shame in ignorance or misunderstanding. Their questions often have us scurrying to Google for answers and will be asked over and over until they are satisfied.

Questions test boundaries as kids seek permission to stretch beyond the confines of their small world. They are often open-ended, with no simple answers. The question itself might be more important than the answer. Children need to know that it is okay to have doubts and be unsure. They are content with mystery and the wonder of a question that cannot be easily answered. Adults need the same kind of freedom.

I am reminded of that as I think about the 1977 movie *The Last Wave*, in which a Sydney lawyer, David Burton, played by Richard Chamberlain, is asked to defend five aborigines accused of the murder of another tribesman. It plunges him into Australian aboriginal dreamtime spirituality. In one poignant scene, David confronts his stepfather, an Anglican priest: "Why didn't you tell me there are mysteries," he asks. Then he shouts, "You stood in that church and explained them away."

God is still a mystery to us. There is much we will never understand, but we need the freedom to question and explore the mysteries of faith.

THE SPIRITUAL PRACTICE OF
ASKING QUESTIONS

In *Becoming Curious: A Spiritual Practice for Asking Questions*, Casey Tygrett points out that questioning can be a form of exploration. He reminds us that Jesus changed the story of the people of God by asking questions.

> The Jesus who changed the world shifted the narrative of God and humans, and he did it by engaging questions. The point of Jesus' questions was to stoke curiosity rather than seeing it as an obstacle or a problem. He was intentional, clever, honest, and

persistent with every question he asked. He invited people to explore and think along with him saying, "If you have ears, listen deeply to this one."[1]

British theologian John Stott gave me permission to return to the curiosity of childhood and ask questions like this again. At a lecture I attended back in the 1980s he commented, "The answers we get depend on the questions we ask." He invited us to view new experiences as opportunities to question faith, life, and God. It was liberating for me.

I had just returned from the refugee camps on the Thai-Cambodian border with many questions about suffering, poverty, and justice, but was discouraged from asking them or searching for answers that could push me beyond my current theological box. Yet that was exactly what God wanted me to do. My God was too small and confining for the journey that lay ahead. My joy in God and in God's purposes for me only returned when I grappled with the questions and found peace in the new and unexpected answers that stretched and enriched my faith.

Sometimes doubts are intensified because we ask the wrong questions. Passive questions that expect God to do something without my active engagement are destructive, not constructive. When I blame God, I don't need to respond. "Why does God allow suffering?" sidesteps my responsibility and sometimes culpability in the situation I am struggling with. Now I replace it with "What does God ask me to do when I am confronted with suffering?" Or "Where is God in the midst of this suffering?"

Jesus often answered questions with questions that invited active responses rather than passive reactions. This encouraged his followers to think, reimagine, and draw on the truths for creative solutions already hidden in their hearts. Curiosity is not just about gaining knowledge but learning how to behave in a complex and confusing world.

Questioning has many purposes.

It enables us to discover new truths. When we admit we don't know something, we open ourselves to new revelations.

Questioning also helps establish boundaries and explore beyond our comfort zone in nonthreatening ways. Surprisingly, the answers may not come from outside but often well up from within us. Thomas Merton calls this the "hidden wholeness," the image of God hidden in our souls.[2]

Questions also remind us that there is still mystery in our world, wisdom beyond understanding that we should embrace rather than dismiss. God is far bigger and far more complex than the scientific explanations we hope for.

My friend Andy Wade helped me ask questions that changed my perspectives and enriched my spiritual life. Like me, he is a passionate gardener, and in the early days of our exploration of garden spirituality we often sparked each others' imaginations and spiritual insights. One day he asked a new question: "What would happen if we designed our gardens with God and neighbor in mind?"

Andy set out to do just that and challenged me to follow suit. He worked on his backyard vegetable garden specifically asking, "What if I redesigned this with God in mind?" *God never creates straight lines*, he surmised. His new beds were curved with broad paths interspersed with places to sit and contemplate. It is an inviting space that I can imagine God wandering through, picking tomatoes, and sitting beside Andy as he works and prays.

Then Andy turned to the front yard specifically asking, "What if I redesigned this with my neighbors in mind?" He removed the front fence, which created a barrier to those who walked past, added a path that wended its way through his herb garden to a comfortable sitting area, added instructions on how to make tea from the plants, and finished it off with a free lending library.

This spiritual practice has had a profound effect on Andy and all who have walked into his garden.[3]

What would happen if we designed our spiritual practices with God and neighbor in mind? What do you love doing that you could frame this same question around? I think we would be amazed at the beautiful practices that result.

Many young mothers I talk to feel closest to God when they nurse their infants. Commuters often experience intimacy with God as they drive to work. Volunteers find closeness to God when they work with the homeless, refugees, or disabled. These can all become profound spiritual experiences in which we sense God's delight.

> WHAT WOULD HAPPEN IF WE DESIGNED OUR SPIRITUAL PRACTICES WITH GOD AND NEIGHBOR IN MIND?

Do your kitchen and cooking stir you to plan with God and neighbor in mind? Perhaps God is prompting you to reimagine your passion as a ministry of hospitality to neighbors or the marginalized in your community. Is your passion for playing or creating music? Perhaps you could plan a neighborhood street concert. Imagine ways that you could shape your passion into an intimate encounter with the divine presence and extend God's love into your community.

WHAT WOULD YOU DO IF YOU WERE NOT AFRAID?

During Lent one year, I used the phrase "Let fear become love" as the focus for my contemplation. I wended my way through a series of questions that transformed my fears for the future into an intimate encounter with the love of God and God's delight in who I am.

I started by asking, *What am I afraid of?* This important question I ask periodically, especially when God prompts me to step outside my comfort zones and explore new boundaries for my faith.

Fear often paralyzes us, thwarting our creativity and stopping us from responding to the curiosity deep within our souls. I hate to disturb the status quo or to disrupt the peace and quiet of my orderly life. Sometimes I am afraid of criticism for stepping outside the box of convention. Whatever my fears, I need to confront them, and questions are a good and often nonthreatening way to do that. They allow the flow of God's creative Spirit to bend around our self-imposed barriers and create a new path for us to follow.

When my friend Heather asked herself, *What am I afraid of?* her fear of disabled people came to mind. To help confront this, she visited the local L'Arche community. Initially, she was alarmed by a high-pitched noise a woman with Down syndrome was making. Then she realized the woman was laughing and expressing joy. Heather's interactions with this woman broke down her fear and transformed it into love.

Heather's friend confessed her fear of Muslims. She visited the local mosque, met the imam's wife, and enjoyed a wonderful conversation over tea and cookies. Here too fear was transformed into love. Neither Heather nor her friend thought of what they did as spiritual practices, but that is certainly what they are. Asking themselves about their fears stirred their creativity, enriched their faith, increased their joy, and brought them closer to both God and their neighbors.

What would I do if I were not afraid? This question challenged me when I confronted my own fear of being alone when I grow old. In some ways it is a legitimate fear. My husband is much older than I am; I have no children, and my family is half a world away in Australia. Yet the Scriptures tell us that perfect love casts out fear. My fear often blinds me to the love of God, and the dread of loneliness paralyzes and isolates me. My fears become self-fulfilling prophesies.

The first step to overcoming our fears is to voice them. Sharing our deepest concerns with others often releases us from the fears that constrict us. Second, we need to do what Merton suggested and reach for the wholeness hidden within. This wholeness is liberating and life changing. This often rises to the surface as we ask ourselves the simple question, *What would I do if I were not afraid?*

If I were not afraid of being alone, I would see that I am never alone because God is always with me. I would nurture a deeper and more intimate relationship with God for the days ahead. If I were not afraid of being alone, I would strengthen friendships, taking time to nurture and appreciate friends and family that still provide love and support.

What about you? If you were not afraid of . . .

What would happen if I allowed love to speak into my fears? This question became an even more profound spiritual practice for me and took several weeks to unpack. It incorporated my own creative response to the first two questions.

I printed out the words *Let fear become love* in large letters in Zenfyrkalt, a beautiful decorative font I found on the internet, then colored one letter each day. I recited "Let fear become love" as I colored, and found the words resonating deep within my soul.

Then I did a Bible search of the word *love*. Using BibleGateway .com, I chose three translations—the New Living Translation, *The Voice*, and the New International Version—read through dozens of verses, comparing the translations and their implications. Two verses held my attention: "Don't lose your grip on [God's] Love and Loyalty. Tie them around your neck; carve their initials on your heart" (Proverbs 3:3 *The Message*). And "Use your freedom to serve one another in love. That's how freedom grows" (Galatians 5:13 *The Message*).

These verses reminded me of Thomas Merton's *Seasons of Celebration*, where he says: "God's People first came into existence when the children of Israel were delivered from slavery in Egypt and called out into the desert to be educated into freedom, to learn how to live with no other master but God himself."[4]

True freedom and love are intertwined. Freedom flows from the heart of our loving God, and it grows as we share. Love that is caring and compassionate stretches across boundaries of hate and animosity, seeking for understanding and forgiveness. God's love grows as we enter into this kind of freedom.

What are your most compelling Q's?

So, curiosity = Questions?

but also allurement.

WHERE IS GOD IN THE MIDST
OF DISASTER?

One challenging question we all struggle with is, Where is God in the midst of disaster? When I wrote this chapter, Hurricane Maria had just devastated Puerto Rico and wildfires raged in California. In India, Bangladesh, and Pakistan forty-one million people were displaced by torrential monsoonal flooding with at least twelve hundred deaths. My heart ached for the thousands who lost homes and livelihood in the midst of these disasters. I was overwhelmed by my inability to respond.

How can I talk about enjoying God while grieving with so many brothers and sisters who have lost loved ones and livelihoods? It is not an easy time for many of us as we question how a loving and caring God could allow such disasters to happen. There are no easy answers. Yet this does not mean that God is absent. Nor does it mean that we cannot enjoy our wonderful God in the midst of disaster.

In *The Book of Joy*, Archbishop Tutu and the Dalai Lama suggest that the way we heal our own pain is actually by turning to the pain of others. Being more joyful is not just about having more fun. "We're talking about a more empathetic, more empowered, more spiritual state of mind that is totally engaged with the world."[5] Thinking about others is a way of handling our worries, partly because it helps us to see ourselves as part of a greater whole.

In *A Paradise Built in Hell*, Rebecca Solnit explains that extraordinary communities arise in the midst of disaster. Calamity doesn't bring out the worst in us, she contends. It brings out the best. Resourcefulness, generosity, and joy arise to shine brightly in the midst of all kinds of horrifying situations. "The joy in disaster comes, when it comes, from an affection that is not private and personal but civic. The love of strangers for each other, of a citizen for his or her city, of belonging to a greater whole, of doing the work that matters."[6]

That's it, I thought as I contemplated this current wave of disasters. *Not why does God allow this, but where do I see God's love expressed?*

Strangers became neighbors. Across barriers of class and race and religion, people showed they care. Amazing! People half a world away dropped everything to risk their lives for someone they don't know and may never see again. The parable of the good Samaritan is being lived out in our midst. Heroic rescues, sacrificial acts, and generous giving are the image of God welling up from within our souls, shining light in the darkness. Why these disasters happened we do not know, but God is there grieving, loving, and caring in and through us.

John O'Donohue articulates this beautifully:

> We carry in us a deep strain of God's caring. Our love for our friends and family, our concern for the world and for the earth, our compassion for the pain and desperation of others are not simply the product of an "unselfish gene" within us, they issue from that strain of God in us that prizes above everything the kindness, the compassion, and the beauty that love brings. Anywhere: in prayer, family, front line, brothel or prison, anywhere care comes alive, God is present.[7]

As these thoughts took shape in my mind, compassion fatigue gave way to compassionate action. My "It's really God's fault" response transformed into an active reaching out. *I can help*, I realized. I can pray. I can give to emergency funds. I can look at options for long-term involvement

WHERE HAVE YOU SEEN CARE AND COMPASSION COME ALIVE RECENTLY AND RECOGNIZED THE LOVING PRESENCE OF GOD?

like a Habitat for Humanity building team. Disaster shakes our complacency to the many devastating events around our globe that we should respond to.

Disaster blots out the sun but allows the light that is within each of us to shine to its full potential, not alone but together with the many other lights that surround us. In the process it gives us direction—a clear path toward the kind of interdependent caring life that God intends for all of us and that is where we find our joy.

Where have you seen care and compassion come alive recently and recognized the loving presence of God?

LET YOUR FINGERS DO THE WALKING

One of my favorite spiritual tools is the labyrinth, especially finger labyrinths. I use mine frequently when pondering questions like the one I just asked. They are used not only for prayer and healing but also to get ready for meetings, to break through writer's block, and to cure insomnia. Labyrinths provide a legitimate pathway for questioning and problem solving. Finger labyrinths can be found in third- and fourth-century churches. Their circuits are well worn by the passage of innumerable fingers "walking on pilgrimage" to the center and out again.

It seems weird, but research suggests that when we trace a finger labyrinth with our nondominant hand, it accesses our intuition and helps stir our creativity.

Much to my surprise, I found that it really works, so you can imagine my delight when I was given a beautiful wooden eleven-circuit labyrinth modeled after the famous one set in the stone floor in the nave of Chartres Cathedral in France. Throughout the writing of this book, my finger labyrinth sat prominently displayed and ready to be used whenever I puzzled over a challenging question.

A growing number of churches and religious institutions, for example, Calvin College, encourage their congregations and students to walk labyrinths during Lent and Holy Week as a meditative walk toward the cross.[8] *Pilgrim Paths* in the United Kingdom has produced an excellent brochure for a Holy Week walk that could easily be adapted for finger labyrinths as an alternative to stations of the cross.[9]

Hospitals and nursing homes too recognize the therapeutic benefits of labyrinths. Some have large and visible ones outdoors, but they are increasingly finding that finger labyrinths are important too. Finger labyrinths are convenient and accessible for patients who are confined to beds or wheelchairs.

What a hodge podge!
Doesn't really stay with
Curiosity.

PRACTICE
Walk a Finger Labyrinth

Creating and walking finger labyrinths is a stimulating exercise. Search Pinterest for inspirational patterns. Print one out on a sheet of paper.[1] Color it, decorate it with symbols or flowers, trickle glue around it, and then sprinkle sand on it to create a raised pattern, or write Bible verses around the pathway. This is a meditative exercise in itself and provides a perfect template for the following exercise.

Sit in a quiet place. Sit in a quiet place with your finger labyrinth in your lap. Take a few breaths in and out until you feel at peace in your soul. Read through the story of Jesus calming the storm (Matthew 14:22-33). Imagine it raging around you and your desire to step outside the boat of convention and ask uncomfortable questions. Visualize Jesus coming toward you holding out his hands and saying, "Don't be afraid of your doubts and your questions. I am with you always." Imagine you are Peter stepping out of the boat into unknown waters.

Recite this prayer. Recite this prayer or a similar prayer of welcome and receptivity: "Walk with me, Lord, through all the twists and turns of life; walk with me when clouds obscure the way, when what seemed close is now so far away. Walk with me, Lord, until I trust in you; lead me to the center of your love."

Form your question. Place a finger from your nondominant hand at the entrance to the labyrinth. Prayerfully ask a question you have struggled with about faith. Invite the Holy Spirit of God to guide and instruct you on your journey.

Trace the circuit with your finger. Stay open to whatever presents itself: feelings, sensations, memories, ideas. Pause at any time to breathe. Stay with a thought or memory or just relax into the labyrinth and the question stirring in your mind. At the center of the labyrinth, sense your connection to your own center and to God's centering presence. Acknowledge the Holy Spirit, the heavenly Counselor directing your thoughts and exploration. Relax, pray, sing. Repeat your question.

Trace your way out. Trace your way out, staying open to whatever comes to you. When your walk is done, place both hands on the labyrinth and sit quietly in the presence of God once more. Thank God for your questioning heart and for the enrichment it brings to your faith.

Trust your gut and the journey it takes you on. Believe in your creative impulses. Is there a solution to your question that surfaces? Write it down. How is God nudging you to respond? Write it down. Are there people you need to talk to? Get out your phone and make an appointment.

Finish with prayer. Offer a prayer of gratitude to God for the responses that have come to you and the power of the Holy Spirit to heal and change you.

HAVE SOME FUN WITH FRIENDS

If you are meeting with a group, either use the finger labyrinth exercise for each participant to create their own finger labyrinth or plan a trip to a local labyrinth, preferably one in a church or its grounds.

Invite each person to walk the labyrinth alone and write their reflections on their experiences.

Get together for a time of sharing. What questions did people ask? What did they experience as they walked the labyrinth? What insights were revealed in response to their questions?

Finish with a time of group prayer.

Curios about ← ideas people places things events

now we see dimly

REMEMBER WE
ARE EARTHLINGS

Lord, I sit at peace,
my feet planted firmly on the earth,
anchored by it, connected through it
to God and to all things living.
My roots grow deep toward the river of life,
drinking from it, nourished by it, linked through it
to the neighbors I journey with, the creation I care for,
the God I love.
My soul is at rest.
God is closer than my heartbeat, deeper than my breath.
I sit in awe and wonder,
accepting this earth, this sky, this water of life
as a gift from God.

My office window looks out over our vegetable garden filled with tomatoes in summer but muddy and barren in winter. It is a favorite place for kids to play. I watch them jump in the puddles, throw mud at each other, and delight in the discovery of earthworms, snails, and other small, unsavory creatures. I am intrigued by their imaginative use of sticks, rocks, and leaves, and laugh at their dirt-smeared, grinning faces.

I think that God loves playing in the dirt too. In the story of our creation in Genesis, God reaches down into the rich, loamy, fragrant soil, teeming with microbes, sculpts it into human form, breathes into it, and gives us life (Genesis 2:7). St. Augustine calls us *terra animate*—animated earth, "soil people, inspired by the breath of God."[1] Humbling and inspiring at the same time—soil people, created from the earth and for the earth.

Then we read, "And the LORD God planted a garden in Eden" (Genesis 2:8 ESV). According to a friend who is both a gardener and Hebrew scholar, the original text implies God got down in the mud, dug in the soil with dirty hands, and planted the most beautiful garden imaginable (Genesis 2:15). Here God the cosmic gardener comes to walk, enjoy, and interact not just with us as caretakers but with all creation (Genesis 3:8). When Adam and Eve sin, they lose not just their intimate relationship with God but also their relationship to the soil they were formed from and their delight in all of God's beautiful creation.

In *Making Peace with the Land*, Norman Wirzba and Fred Bahnson explain:

> God's first love is the soil. This is how it has to be, because without healthy soil and the fertility and food it makes possible, there would be no terrestrial life of any kind. God's love for us—described definitely in John 3:16 as God's giving of his son to us—only makes sense in terms of God's love for the earth that sustains us.[2]

I wonder is the love of the soil part of our DNA? There is nothing quite like getting hands in the soil, savoring the aroma of rich, fertile earth, or even just playing in the mud. Kids love it, and a lot of adults do too.

One way to pray that really gets us in touch with the soil and its God-loved goodness is to shed our shoes and socks and walk through a patch of grass, bare soil, mud puddle, or even the sand on the beach. As the cool grass embraces my feet and soil or sand oozes up between my toes, I am reminded of nineteenth-century poet Gerald Manley Hopkin's wonderful poem "God's Grandeur." "The world is charged with the grandeur of God," he exclaims, but then goes on to remind us "the soil is bare now, nor can foot feel, being shod."

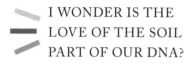

I WONDER IS THE LOVE OF THE SOIL PART OF OUR DNA?

There is something amazingly spiritual about walking barefoot through a patch of God's good earth. Our toes tingle with new sensations that are as soothing as an expensive massage. Then I step on a prickle. Ouch, it hurts. All is not perfect here. I need to be attentive and take notice of what could cause pain, of where there is still brokenness in both our world and my own life. I offer a prayer for forgiveness and healing.

ARE WE SUFFERING FROM NATURE DEFICIT DISORDER?

Unfortunately, we have become strangers to the soil—with dire consequences for our physical, spiritual, and emotional health. Richard Louv, author of *Last Child in the Woods*, calls this "nature-deficit disorder."[3] He argues that all of us, especially children, spend more time indoors, which alienates us from nature and makes us vulnerable to negative moods and reduces our attention span. Florence Williams in her fascinating article *This Is Your Brain on Nature*, in which she recounts a trip into the wilds of Utah with cognitive psychologist David Strayer suggests that "Science is proving what we've always known intuitively: nature does good things to the human brain—it makes us healthier, happier, and smarter."[4] When we get out into nature, according to David Strayer, something profound happens. "When we slow down, stop the busywork, and take in beautiful natural surroundings, not only do we feel restored, but our mental performance improves too."[5]

Just living near nature dramatically improves health. Contact with nature helps children develop cognitive and intellectual skills and social relationships while encouraging imagination and creativity. Symptoms of attention deficit hyperactivity disorder (ADHD) can be alleviated by spending time outside. The whole Finnish school system embraces this principle, and now schools in Oklahoma, Texas, and California are tripling recess time with the same favorable results.[6]

Some researchers even suggest that exposure to dirt increases happiness, and sniffing compost gives us a physical high. No kidding, for some people it is as intoxicating as alcohol or drugs! To top it off, eating dirt improves our immune systems. Too much cleanliness is not next to godliness. It creates an imbalance of the millions of microbes in our bodies and might contribute to the increased incidence of asthma, allergies, and autoimmune disorders.[7] It seems we not only need to encourage our kids to go out, get dirty, and eat a little dirt, we need to get out there and play in the dirt with them.

I suspect this profound impact of communing with nature goes far deeper than the health of body, mind, and soul. It is fundamentally connected to our "kinship with the divine."[8] We are made in the image of God, who through imagination and creativity delighted in bringing into being all of creation.

I love what Irish poet John O'Donohue says about this.

Everything that is—every tree, bird, star, stone and wave—existed first as a dream in the mind of the divine artist. Indeed the world is the mirror of the divine imagination and to decipher the depths of the world is to gain deep insights into the heart of God. The traces of the divine imagination are everywhere. The beauty of God becomes evident in the beauty of the world.[9]

Ironically, the recession of 2008 got many of us back into the dirt. An amazing community-garden network, which I believe was a mighty move of God, swept across the North American continent as urban dwellers like me planted gardens to cut back on food budgets. As our taste buds exploded with the sweet flavor of tomatoes straight from the vine and corn picked and immediately thrown in the cooking pot, many of us became obsessed with converting our lawns into edible vegetation. Our whole front yard has now become a garden, and I am always looking for more space to plant in. Salad made straight from the garden or leeks and carrots pulled from the frosty ground are better than anything dished up in a five-star restaurant.

Digging in the soil, we discovered, relieves our stress and opens our eyes to God's glory and majesty in all creation. Like kids, we started to see beauty in the most unexpected places. Dandelions, weeds in the cracks, even moss on the wall suddenly became breathtaking revelations of God, who is still planting gardens in surprising places.

The psalmists were very aware of this. In Psalm 65:9-13 we read,

> You take care of the earth and water it,
>   making it rich and fertile.
> The river of God has plenty of water;
>   it provides a bountiful harvest of grain,
>   for you have ordered it so.
> You drench the plowed ground with rain,
>   melting the clods and leveling the ridges.
> You soften the earth with showers
>   and bless its abundant crops.
> You crown the year with a bountiful harvest;
>   even the hard pathways overflow with abundance.
> The grasslands of the wilderness become a lush pasture,
>   and the hillsides blossom with joy.
> The meadows are clothed with flocks of sheep,
>   and the valleys are carpeted with grain.
>   They all shout and sing for joy! (NLT)

Early Christians were also aware of this connection. They believed that God spoke through two books—the Bible and creation. Celtic Christians in the sixth century saw creation as translucent, with the glory of God shining through it. This view is reflected in the writings of the great Irish teacher John Scotus Eriugena, who taught that God speaks through the physical little book, the book of Scripture, and the big book, the book of creation, vast as the universe.

Modern-day Celtic scholar Phillip Newell explains,

> Eriugena invites us to listen to the two books in stereo. He encourages us to listen to the strains of the human heart in scripture and to discern within them the sound of God and to listen to the murmurings and thunders of creation and to know within them the music of God's being. To listen to the one without the other is to only half listen. To listen to scripture without creation is to lose the cosmic vastness of the song. To listen to creation without scripture is to use the personal intimacy of the voice. . . . In the Celtic world, both texts are read in the company of Christ.[10]

This appears to be what the community-garden movement reawakened us to. We were familiar with the God revealed in the Bible, but now, suddenly we're overwhelmed by God's glory shining through creation and it was exciting.

THEY PLANTED HIM IN A GARDEN

Earth day, April 22, commemorating the founding of the modern environmental movement, is increasingly seen by churches and creation-care organizations as an opportunity to reconnect their congregations to God's love for creation. It often beautifully coincides with Easter and our celebrations of the death and resurrection of Christ. In fact, the journey of Holy Week can be seen as a journey back into the garden of God. The imagery in the Gospel of John is particularly vivid in portraying this.

Jesus' suffering begins in the garden of Gethsemane, the day before his crucifixion. In this garden his agony is poured out in drops of blood, like sweat, that seep into the earth. His pain is symbolic of the pain and suffering that became a part of Adam and Eve's lives when they were expelled from the garden of Eden.

On Good Friday there is another garden. Jesus, the second Adam, dies at Golgotha and John notes, "In the place where he was crucified there was a garden" (John 19:41 KJV). Here Jesus' body is placed. His death is like the planting of a seed, reminding us that "I tell you the truth, unless a kernel of wheat is planted in the soil and dies, it remains alone. But its death will produce many new kernels—a plentiful harvest of new lives" (John 12:24 NLT).

In 1511 the German artist Albrecht Dürer fashioned a woodcut of Mary Magdalene's encounter with the resurrected Jesus as depicted in John 20:15. She came to the garden tomb looking for Christ's body, instead she found a very much alive Jesus, and "she thought he was the gardener." This is not a throwaway phrase. It is of cosmic significance! Jesus is indeed a gardener. He is the gardener of the new creation. Here in this garden that begins in death, new life emerges and the glory of God is revealed.

The Genesis story begins in a garden paradise and ends in our present garden world of pain and suffering. The Easter story begins in the garden of pain and suffering and ends in a garden of wholeness and flourishing, a new paradise in which we, abundantly provided for, once more walk close to our God.

I love this imagery. It sends goose bumps through my body. In this new garden Jesus, the head gardener, once more invites us to be who God created us to be—stewards of all creation, tending this new paradise so that it once more flourishes for all the creatures of the earth to enjoy.

In Isaiah 65 and again in Revelation 21 we see beautiful pictures of this new garden of God. Life and freedom, wholeness and abundance flourish, and we look forward in hope to its completion.

Our challenge is cooperating with Jesus the gardener in his work. In many ways God's new garden is still in its infancy and needs care in order to flourish. Soil must be fertilized, seeds planted, watered, and nurtured, fruit harvested. To see it completed, we must willingly journey with Jesus from the garden of Gethsemane with its struggle and suffering, through the garden of death to the new life that begins in the garden of the resurrection.

The old Adam and Eve were excluded from Eden by a barrier of angels with flaming swords. Jesus, the new Adam, ripped apart the barrier with his death and stands ready to welcome us into the new paradise garden. The barrier that separated us from the holy place of intimacy with God and God's world has been removed. Now, together with all God's people and indeed with all God's creation, we can enter into the intimacy of relationship with God in a restored world of wholeness and abundance. We must continue to till and fertilize the soil, and plant seeds of freedom and generosity and wholeness until the full glory of God's resurrection-created world is revealed.

One beautiful practice some of my friends and their kids love to create at Easter is a resurrection garden. All you need is a terra cotta tray, a small terra cotta pot for the tomb, and some potting soil and small pebbles to create the garden. Plant grass seed on top of the tomb, place a large rock in front, and craft twigs into crosses. Water daily and watch it flourish. This is an easy project, even if you don't have a green thumb.[11] It is a wonderful expression of the connections between the Easter story and God's good creation.

Resurrection gardens inspired me to create meditation gardens for all the seasons of the liturgical calendar. Planning, creating, and then using gardens for Advent, Lent, and Easter in particular has strengthened my faith and revealed new depths of the joy in God's heart. I often say, "I read about the story of God in the Bible, but in nature I experience it." All gardens are living parables: life, death, and resurrection lived out daily. Reading the story reflected in God's garden reaffirms our faith and enriches us with new perspectives on the God we love.

In the last ten years many churches have converted their green grass or parking lots into community gardens or looked for ways to invite neighbors into their green space. One church I worked with invited the congregation into the garden once a month after the morning service to help weed and tend the crops. They finished with a lunch featuring salad greens straight from the soil. Another made gardening part of the youth group responsibility. Still another held children's church in the garden once a month. It was fun to watch teenagers and toddlers who had never eaten a fresh vegetable not only weed the beans and broccoli but eat them raw.

Churches aren't the only institutions who have discovered the delight of gardening and rejoiced the heart of God through their endeavors. Prisons, relief organizations, and programs for returning war vets are planting gardens too. They are discovering that their clientele finds healing through digging in the earth. One of our favorite movies is *Greenfingers*, a delightful story with Clive Owen and Helen Mirren. Clive is in prison for murdering his brother. He thinks that he will never be free. Then he and a group of other hardened criminals are told to plant a garden as part of an experimental plan to rehabilitate them. Watching the transformation that takes place in their lives is heartwarming.

Gardening also creates a deeper sense of community with neighbors. When a church plants a garden in its front yard, passersby experience the congregation's concern for their community. Sometimes people stop and talk and are drawn into the church fellowship as well.

In our own small intentional community we grow about 40 percent of our fruit and vegetables. We invite neighbors and friends who have no gardens to join our monthly garden days, and once a year we hold an apple party, inviting friends and strangers to join us in processing our two hundred pounds of apples. Not only do we share garden techniques, we also learn about God, faith, and what it means to be followers of Christ.

This garden enthusiasm has become one of my richest spiritual prompts, inspiring me to write my own prayers and liturgies of glory to God. It also birthed "Spirituality of Gardening" seminars to help congregations connect their faith and their garden experiences. Here is one of my favorite liturgies, first published in my book *To Garden with God*.

God bless this garden
Through which your glory shines,
May we see in its beauty the wonder of your love.
God bless the soil
Rich and teeming with life,
May we see in its fertility the promise of new creation.
God bless our toil
As we dig deep to turn the soil,
May we see in our labour your call to be good stewards.
God bless each seed
That takes root and grows,
May we see in their flourishing the hope of transformation.
God bless the rains
That water our efforts to bring forth life,
May we see in their constancy God's faithful care.
God bless the harvest
Abundant and bountiful in season,
May we see in God's generosity our need to share.
God bless this garden
As you bless all creation with your love,
May we see in its glory your awesome majesty.[12]

Gardening also teaches us about God's economic views of over-whelming abundance. It encourages us to share and be generous.

I noticed this during the Great Recession. People who planted vegetable gardens were transformed from hoarders to sharers. The exploding bounty that came from planting small seeds inspired them to believe there really is enough for everyone. Seed multiplies; fruit grows and flourishes. We no longer want to hold on to everything, because we realize that our generous God has indeed given us enough for our own needs and an abundance to share. Gifts to food banks and community kitchens and sharing with friends and neighbors in harvest celebrations are but a few ways churches share the bounty they produce. So make sure that you plan at least one garden party this year where the garden produce has pride of place in the food on the table.

Finally, I think we understand 2 Corinthians 9:10-11:

> The same One who has put seed into the hands of the sower and brought bread to fill our stomachs will provide and multiply the resources you invest and produce an abundant harvest from your righteous actions. You will be made rich in everything so that your generosity *will spill over in every direction. Through us* your generosity is at work inspiring praise and thanksgiving to God.

Many aspects of God's creation inspire us to pray. Applying childlike playfulness, curiosity, and creativity enriches our godly encounters as we imagine elephants in the clouds or gaze at the breathtaking array of stars on a moonless night. The sound of wind through the trees evokes images of the Holy Spirit. Cascading music of water over rocks awakens the voice of God. I brush against my lavender or basil and the aroma floods my nostrils with a banquet of goodness. I crush leaves between my fingers and am reminded of Revelation 8:4: "The smoke of the incense mixed with the prayers of God's people and billowed up before God." I walk in the rain, and the fresh smell of ozone in the air raises my spirits. The whole creation joins in my prayer, with all the senses of sight, touch, smell, sound, and taste, and that in itself fills me with wonder and joy.

One effective way to apply this is through the practice of *lectio tierra* an adaptation of lectio divina to nature. I was introduced to it at a retreat on Celtic spirituality a couple of years ago. Listening to the speaker, I realized that I have practiced it for years, I just didn't know what to call it. As I wander through the forest, admire the growing zucchini in my garden, harvest beans, or breathe the sweet fragrance of lavender, I enter a meditative process that opens me to the awe and wonder of God's world.

Like lectio divina, lectio tierra begins with reading.[13] I head into God's good creation with the deliberate intention of "reading" where God is present and what God is saying. *What might God use to catch my eye and draw me closer?* is a good beginning question. Anything that catches my attention provides fuel for reflection. I can discern its story, discover the intersections of that story with my own story, and sit in harmony with it. My eyes might be drawn to an old oak tree, a leaf falling from the tree, or the sound of water trickling down a hillside. I stop, look, and listen, not forcing a revelation but waiting in the silence for God to nudge me in a definite direction. What story do I discern? How might it speak to me of God?

Now I meditate. I gasp in awe at the pattern of bark, interweaving like Celtic braiding. My eyes are drawn to the blackened scars that speak of fire damage. The tree has survived in spite of its traumatic past and in some ways is stronger and more full of life as a result. The fire burned off undergrowth that prevented nourishment from reaching the roots. The nearby stream forced its roots to grow deeper and draw from the hidden wellsprings of life beneath the surface. Psalm 1 comes to me: "You are like a tree, planted by *flowing, cool* streams of water *that never run dry*" (Psalm 1:3).

I pray, touching the scars and smelling the fragrance of the leaves. I reflect on the blackened scars of my own life that are still present. They too have contributed to the strength and resilience of who I am becoming. I thank God for the deep roots that continue to grow into the water that will never run dry. I ask for insight into other scars that are still weeping and need to be sealed. I pray for God's peace and guidance that I may continue to grow tall and strong in God's garden world.

The last step is contemplation. I pause, running my hands along the braided pattern on the trunk, feeling the roughness of the bark beneath my fingers. I observe the other trees in the forest and know I am not alone. I breathe in and absorb the insights God has given, enabling me to move into a place of peace. I can grow strong and tall in spite of my scars and past traumas. I can receive love, healing, and grace from God and continue to grow into the person God intends me to be. I feel at one with God's world and with the people that help move me toward God's wholeness.

EARTH DAY ECO AUDIT

A Rocha Canada calls the Sunday after Earth Day "Good Seed Sunday." They provide excellent resources that encourage congregations to honor their Creator and God's good creation on this day.[14]

Last year I had the delight of conducting a "Spirituality of Gardening" seminar at Cedar Park Church in Ladner, BC, as part of their Earth Day celebrations. We ended the morning by making seed bombs.[15] This is one of my favorite Earth Day activities. Seed bombs are made with clay, compost, and seed, and then thrown into abandoned lots, toxic waste fields, even potholes. It was both a fun and instructive day. We all enjoyed getting our hands dirty while learning more about our God and this beautiful world we live in.

The following day, Good Seed Sunday, Tom and I preached about God's love for creation and the ways that the environmental movement had influenced both of us. The pastor shared how he spent Saturday afternoon with his daughter surreptitiously dropping seed bombs in places where they hoped wildflowers would grow. He particularly enjoyed being able to throw bombs of peace and life rather than death and destruction. After church there was a plant swap, and I wished I could sneak a few plants across the border with me back to Seattle.

There are other ways to encourage our churches to be more responsible stewards of creation that may not seem like spiritual practices but I feel are really important for strengthening our faith and regaining our role as God's stewards.

Consider doing an eco audit of your church as part of your Earth Day celebration next year. Operation Noah has developed an extensive list of questions that can help us evaluate how green our churches are, not just in their use of energy but in their worship focus too.[16] Recruit your kids to check out which light bulbs need to be replaced and to set up compost piles and recycling bins. How green is your church? Could you do an eco audit as part of your responsibility to creation stewardship?

When our church asked "How green is our church?" a few years ago, it led to a lot of changes in how things are done.

> HOW GREEN IS YOUR CHURCH? COULD YOU DO AN ECO AUDIT AS PART OF YOUR RESPONSIBILITY TO CREATION STEWARDSHIP?

We started using recyclable plates and cups at coffee hour, composted all waste food to use in the vegetable garden that sprang up in the church grounds, and added solar panels to some of the buildings. It's amazing to watch the energy consumption going backward at certain times of the day. It is also satisfying to know that the produce from the garden is used for the monthly Jubilee dinners that provide meals for the homeless.

PRACTICE
Seed Bomb Our Neighborhoods

I love the concept of bombs of peace rather than of war, and seed bombs are something all of us can make no matter how black a thumb we have.

Gather a few basic supplies. Gather a small bag of potting soil and a packet of wildflower seeds appropriate for your area (obtainable at your local nursery). You also need a container of air-dry clay, or you can make your own as part of your activity.

Begin with prayer. Read Psalm 65:9-13, preferably from the New Living Translation. This is one of my favorite "farming" psalms and a good one to read as we think about planting seeds.

Make some air-dry clay. While you reflect on the psalm, make your air-dry clay.

Mix together two cups of baking soda and one cup of cornstarch in a small pot. Add 1 1/4 cups of water and mix until there are no lumps. Heat the dough, stirring constantly until it thickens and is hard to move the whisk through. Cool in a small bowl covered with a wet cloth. Knead the dough (preferably with your hands) until it is smooth.

Clean your hands, pull out your journal, and make some notes. What images or thoughts came to you as you read the psalm and kneaded the dough?

Make your seed bombs. Mix the seed, clay, and compost together in a bowl to a ratio of three handfuls of clay, five handfuls of compost, and one of seed. Knead the mix until the seed is evenly distributed throughout.

Carefully add water, mixing it all together until you get a consistency that you can form into balls about one inch in diameter. Lay them out to bake dry on a sunny windowsill for at least three hours. They may take up to forty-eight hours to be completely dry.

What thoughts came to mind as you participated in this act of creation?

Prepare your attack. Read the description in Revelation 22:1-2 of the new garden city God is creating.

> My heavenly guide brought me to the river of *pure* living waters, *shimmering* as brilliantly as crystal. It flowed out from the throne of God and of the Lamb, flowing down the middle and dividing the street of the holy city. On each bank of the river stood the tree of life, *firmly planted*, bearing twelve kinds of fruit and producing its sweet crop every month *throughout* the year. And the *soothing* leaves that grew on the tree *of life* provided precious healing for the nations.

Think about your own city or town and go for a walk around your neighborhood. Are there places that that could be healed or made beautiful by planting seeds?

Targets for seed bombing should not be privately owned contaminated land, derelict and depressing as they seem. The same for parks and other people's gardens (unless you get permission). In the United Kingdom, beautifying a public space is regarded as criminal damage, so check your own local rules and regulations first.

Seed bombs are most fun when thrown into neglected roundabouts, civic spaces, flowerbeds, and neglected planters. Lob a bomb from a bicycle, a car window, or when passing on foot. And just as nature spreads seed at certain times of the year, so our seed bombs are most effective in spring and autumn, or when we plan our attacks to coincide with heavy rainfall.

Reflect, restore, be transformed. In some parts of the world, hunger is seasonal. It often occurs late in winter when stored food is used up. The imagery in Revelation 22:2 of crops throughout the year is imagery of hope for abundant provision for all people and in all seasons.

Take time to reflect on this and on your experience of seed bombing. What were your thoughts as you bombed your neighborhood? What insights about your neighborhood did it give you?

Now think about your life and the brown areas that need to be healed and revitalized. What has God said to you about these through this experience?

End with prayer and thanksgiving.

HAVE SOME FUN WITH FRIENDS

Seed bombing is a great community activity. Planning and executing it with friends, small groups, or your kids is extremely satisfying. You might like to break this into two sessions—one to make the bombs and one after people have thrown them around the neighborhood.

Before your session, designate one person to visit your local nursery and gather garden supplies. Designate a second person to purchase the air-dry clay. If you want to make it yourself, designate at least two people for this activity. Have one read the psalm while the others make the clay. Another person should research local laws about where you can and cannot throw your bombs.

Set up a table outside where a little mess doesn't matter. Spread out your supplies. What initial thoughts come to mind as you begin this adventure?

Make your seed bombs and discuss where you plan to throw them. Read Psalm 65:9-13, preferably from the New Living Translation. What comes to mind as you think about planting seeds?

Send everyone out to throw their bombs around.

When you regather, have a time of quiet reflection and journaling, then share as a group.

What about this exercise most affected you? What were your thoughts as you bombed your neighborhood? What insights about your neighborhood and about God did it give you?

RETURN TO THE RHYTHM
OF LIFE

Faithful God,
God of rhythm and balance,
Creator of all times and seasons,
fill us with the flow of life,
rest, work, and enjoyment.
Caring God,
God of fun and festivity,
Creator of all that is good and beautiful,
surround us with your delight,
laughter, and play and fun.
Generous God,
God of life and love,
Creator of all that is, all that was, and all that will be,
enrich us with your joy.
May we dance with the angels,
and shout with the children.
May we sing with all creation
of the wonder of God's love.

Imagine what our lives would be like if they flowed to the rhythm God
intends for us. Imagine what a sustainable pace that allows time for

work and rest, solitude and community, fasting, feasting, and fun would look like. Working in the garden and observing nature has given me permission to relax into a different pace of life, a pace that is reflected in the seasons of creation around us.

In *The Seasons of Hope: Empowering Faith Through the Practice of Hope*, Ray Anderson comments, "When we become strangers to the earth we have lost more than our roots; we have lost touch with the rhythm of life."[1] I think it's true. Our disconnect from God's creation has also disconnected us from the rhythm of life God intends for us—rhythms that give us joy and satisfaction and provide time for relaxation and laughter, just like the rhythms of a child's life does. Yet as Ecclesiastes 3:1-2 so succinctly expresses it,

> For everything there is a season,
>   a time for every activity under heaven,
> a time to be born and a time to die,
>   a time to plant and a time to harvest. (NLT)

My body responds to these patterns woven through all creation. It wants to slow down in winter and speed up in summer. When I ignore this I fall into the busy trap of overwork, stress, and burnout again. Recognizing these rhythms and admitting they are God designed and God intended has been liberating for me.

We easily forget that church traditions were originally shaped around the seasonal rhythms of the created world. Advent wreaths probably originated in northern Europe, where roads were impassable in winter and farmers hung their wagon wheels on the walls during this season. They started decorating them then, hanging candles on them for additional light.

The garden year has two seasons of rest and two of frantic activity that are mirrored in the liturgical seasons. We think of spring as the season of planting, but in God's world seed is scattered at the end of the year as seed heads mature and burst. Then it rests. Covered by a wintery coat it waits until the warmth of spring brings it to life. This is Advent, Christmas, and Epiphany—seasons of waiting, hoping, and new beginnings. Winter is a time of preparation, when roots go down deep and pruning is done.

Spring is probably the busiest time in the garden. We plant, weed, fertilize, and mulch. We spend as much time as possible getting our garden ready for the coming season of growth, blossom, and fruit. This is Lent, Easter, and Pentecost. To be honest, growing up in Australia, where Easter comes in autumn, it was hard to imagine the resurrection of Christ when everything around me was dying. My first Easter in the northern hemisphere was a joyful revelation. I watched the daffodils wave their sunny heads in the air and delighted in the tulips, all the colors of the rainbow, emerging through the cold, hard earth. I sang and danced as cherry trees burst into bloom and green leaves unfurled all around me. They filled me with the hope of Christ's resurrection. *This is what it's all about*, I realized. Death does give way to resurrection life. Easter does prepare me to take God's ways out into the world.

In summer we see vigorous growth, a riot of colorful flowers, and rich fruit develop. Surprisingly, this too is a season of rest—this time a rest of enjoyment and satisfaction. There are no major feasts on the liturgical calendar, but this is a season when we watch what we have planted mature, taking credit for it but really having little to do to bring it into being.

Autumn is the next busy season, when the full harvest overwhelms us with it is abundance. We work furiously to eat, preserve, and store all that appears. We recruit friends and share harvest celebrations, and then we collapse exhausted and grateful for the resting of winter months.

Mary DeJong, ecotheologian and cofounder of Friends of Cheasty Greenspace in Seattle, has developed a fascinating monthly practice that helps her exercise her senses and connect to the divine rhythms within creation. She creates a nature mandala from the garden elements present during that month. Her monthly creations awaken her to the changing landscape around her and open all her senses to the beauty of God present in a different way in every season.

Mandala is the Sanskrit word for circle. Both Hinduism and Buddhism use mandalas as artistic ways to represent the spiritual universe for them. They are, however, increasingly created by Christians as meditative exercises to draw them closer to God.

Mary finds that her mandala creation attunes her to what is residing and growing in her environment. As she slowly walks around the house and neighborhood gathering materials, she notices what is sprouting, what is flourishing, and what is dying. Leaves, flowers, sticks, and pine cones can all be arranged into beautiful circular designs. These richly varied offerings open her eyes to the vast biodiversity she lives in. She names each plant in her mandala, all of which have much to offer by way of food, medicine, or crosscultural understanding.

Mary told me that learning about our homescapes in this way doesn't just invite us into more intentional knowledge and understanding of God but also of those we share life and resources with.[2]

PRAYING THROUGH THE SEASONS

Observing, contemplating, and praying through the seasons has put me in touch with the cycle of life and the assurance of hope and resurrection that God has woven through creation. Each season has its own revelations that strengthen our faith and draw us closer to the God we love.

Have you ever wondered how trees survive wintery blasts or why an early warm spell followed by a freeze kills trees that survive far colder weather in the heart of winter? I certainly wondered about this after we almost lost our peach trees to an early freeze a few years ago.

The answer provides an astounding, powerful lesson for our faith. Trees are immovable. They have no choice but to face everything winter throws at them, yet the cold northern realms are populated with huge forests and tall trees.

A tree prepares for winter long before the icy blasts. In autumn as days shorten, chemical reactions in the tree signal the need to slow down, stop growing, and get ready. This is what produces the vibrant colors of autumn. Deciduous trees set buds that contain next year's leaves and flowers and then go dormant, at least above ground. Roots continue to grow, strengthening the tree as they search out water not yet frozen. If buds start growing prematurely, they are destroyed by the icy blasts winter still holds in store, and next year's growth is stunted. The tree might starve and die. That's what happened to our peach tree. It almost died and had no fruit for three years.

A winter-hardy tree even knows how to cope with the destructive freezing water that can send sharp penetrating icicles through cell membranes. As winter approaches, sugar content in cells increases dramatically, and its membrane becomes more flexible—a natural sugary antifreeze that embraces the precious cell contents and keeps it safe until spring. Maple syrup is a particularly good example of this, and I am glad God created it.

How awe-inspiring the creativity and adaptability of God's creation is. I was inspired. I made a quick trip to the fridge and pulled out our bottle of maple syrup. I looked at its beautiful rich amber color. I poured out a spoonful and tasted its goodness. *Maybe French toast and maple syrup need to become a regular part of my "winter" diet*, I thought. Maybe I need to adopt it as a reminder of the sugary sweetness that God uses to prepare us for the wintery blasts in our lives.

Why not take a few minutes to reminisce about the last winter season of your life. Make yourself some pancakes or French toast. Pull out the maple syrup or its equivalent and reflect as you eat. What was the "sugary sweetness" that formed in your life during this season?

How does God want us to prepare for the winter blasts that inevitably come to our lives? Are there spiritual practices that speak of God's ongoing "sugary sweetness"? How could you use these to prepare for the next winter season of your life?

Unfortunately, we rarely embrace the signs that winter is approaching without protest. We resist hunkering down and don't allow our spirits to rest. It is hard for us to let go of the drive to keep growing and producing. We don't want to form buds that must hibernate for a season before germinating, flowering, and fruiting. Sometimes we get impatient and try to force our flowers to bloom too soon. We don't want to hear God say, "Not yet, wait for spring and the new year coming. Enjoy the sweet, sugary embrace of my protective presence. Allow your roots to grow down to the deep water that you will need for the coming season. Enjoy the peace of a world at rest."[3]

> HOW DOES GOD WANT US TO PREPARE FOR THE WINTER BLASTS THAT INEVITABLY COME TO OUR LIVES?

As so often happens when I contemplate like this, a prayer/poem bubbles up within me, filling me with delight.

God prepare us for the winters of our lives.
May we not forget
that hidden within winter's dark embrace
are the seeds of life.
Remind us, loving God, that when all seems dark and empty,
you are still at work,
strengthening our roots,
healing our wounds,
anchoring our souls.
Remind us, generous God,
that when spring dawns,
it is the winter's long rest
that has sustained and nurtured our souls.
Keep us, faithful God,

through the dark journey of life,
so that when a new spring breaks
our roots will be deep and strong.[4]

When spring emerges, different lessons come to life with it. It's
time for new growth and transformation, and by the grace of God I
can join in. In the garden I till the soil, load it with compost, and plant
seeds in its depths. Other seeds have already germinated after their
winter hibernation. I admire the early crocuses and snowdrops, and
gasp in awe at the beaming daffodils and the brightly colored tulips.

Each seed is a promise filled with hope. I plant in the hope that it
will germinate and burst into new life, and as it does so, my joy
is complete.

There are other promises that spring planting brings. In many
countries starvation and hunger are seasonal. In early spring, when the
stored harvest is depleted, poor families rely on dried seeds, nuts, and
beans. They eke out a living with the hope that the new harvest will
begin before their stores are finished.

Each seed planted carries a longing not just for the new growth but
for the firstfruits, the first sprouts that can be eaten and renew life. The
depths of hopelessness is when drought forces a family to use seeds
that are kept for planting as food to survive, forcing themselves into
hunger and starvation for next year too.

In my heart I too long for the germination of new life from seeds
that have been planted in my soul. I long to see the new sprouts, the
promise of a new harvest that I begin to catch glimpses of as the soil
around me warms, softens, and encourages seeds to germinate.

How often, when feeling malnourished after a season of spiritual drought,
do I eat seeds God wants me to plant? How often, I wonder, *have I denied*
God the ability to grow a new and fruitful crop in my heart?

The giving of firstfruits in cultures that live on the edge of starvation during the season between planting and harvest must have been

a huge sacrifice, an incredible denial of their own needs for nourishment so their commitment to God could be fed and nourished first. Maybe that is what the denial of Lent is meant to be about. This is indeed a season to put the needs of God, of others, and of the creation before our own. This is the season above all else when we should nourish the seeds of God's transformation and allow them to grow and flourish. It is time to build up the soil in our personal lives and in our churches. Spring—Lent—is the season for hard spiritual work, intense Scripture study, and discipleship training.

One Lenten discipline we practiced for several years that made us aware of our abundance and helped us identify with the poor and hungry in our world was "the $2 challenge."

For a week during Lent we restricted our food budget to $2 per person per day. It wasn't easy, but it was certainly enlightening.

First, we realized what a difference it makes when we get "free" food from our garden. It certainly stretched our budget and increased the variety. Second, eating in community helped. Each person took responsibility for one evening meal during the week. That freed up time for each of us to do some serious biblical study. Third, realizing that many people always lived on this restricted budget was sobering, and at the end of the week we had a sizable gift to contribute to one of our favorite organizations that worked to end food shortage.

Where has God planted seeds in your life that need to be nurtured until they sprout? Where have you failed to plant seeds because of a scarcity mentality, feeling that you will starve if you keep back some for next year's harvest? And where have we all failed to give God the firstfruits because of our greed?

> WHERE HAS GOD PLANTED SEEDS IN YOUR LIFE THAT NEED TO BE NURTURED UNTIL THEY SPROUT?

The hot, dry days of summer are essentially a respite for gardeners. We mop our brows and sit back, relax, and enjoy the beauty of God's activity. All the backbreaking work of turning the soil and weeding is behind us. There is plenty of time to sit in the sun, listen to the bees, and inhale the fragrance of God's creation.

I love early morning garden walks. I excitedly examine my beans and zucchini to see how they have grown and eye the tomatoes ripening on the vines. Evidently, they do grow more quickly overnight too. Through photosynthesis they absorb energy during the day and then get to work after sunset. I am reminded that for the Jews the day begins at sunset, when we head to bed, but God is working hard. Morning reveals the fruit of God's efforts and invites us to join in.

I am humbled as I remember Paul's words in 1 Corinthians 3:7: "It's not important who does the planting, or who does the watering. What's important is that God makes the seed grow" (NLT). Without our Creator God, our efforts mean nothing. No matter how diligently we plant and water, without God to grow the seed there will never be fruit. *Relax*, I think. *It is time for God to get to work!*

In ministry as well as in the garden, we plant, water, and weed. Then we should relax and watch what God grows. The fruits of our efforts would not be possible without the God who gives them growth. What seeds have you planted in your life or ministry that God is growing? How do you relax and enjoy that growth?

My view of summer spirituality has undergone a radical change in the last few years as I contemplated it as God's season for relaxation and fun. I used to get concerned because so many followers of Jesus seemed to leave their spirituality behind when they went on vacation. Then it occurred to me that I was offering them the wrong kind of summer spirituality.

I asked myself, *What fun things am I planning for the summer that might connect me to Jesus and bring joy to my soul?* I looked over my calendar. There were outdoor concerts and trips to the beach on my agenda. There were BBQs with friends and visits to some of my favorite places. It's a great time to reconnect with people I have not seen for years and find out how God has been moving in their lives.

There were also self-imposed deadlines on projects and a lot of busyness. Some of this would probably be more soul destroying than joy bringing, I realized. I extended the deadlines and gave myself some space for fun.

Summer spirituality could be as simple as flying a kite and thinking about the wind of the Spirit that blows through my life just as the wind blows through this kite, often sending me to somewhere I do not expect.

WHAT FUN THINGS AM I PLANNING FOR THE SUMMER THAT MIGHT CONNECT ME TO JESUS AND BRING JOY TO MY SOUL?

Sometimes there is more intentionality to summer spirituality. When Tom and I talked about our upcoming vacation, we decided to set aside a couple of days for retreat—joy-giving, soul-enriching, and fun. On another occasion when we were in England, we researched the oldest churches in the area and kept a day for a mini-pilgrimage. One church dated back to the twelfth century. Its stone effigies of knights and their wives were fascinating. Reflecting on how God had been present in their lives and in those of their descendants for many generations was a soul-enriching experience.

Finally, autumn comes. This is the season for feasting, celebrating, and enjoying the harvest. The tomatoes and squash ripen, the figs and pears are harvested, and we wait hopefully for a bumper crop of apples. The flavors of fruit and vegetables fresh from the garden are a delight. Food as God intended it to be. "Taste and see that the LORD is good" (Psalm 34:8 NLT). *How do we taste and savor the flavor of God*, I wonder?

Tom and I both love to cook special meals for friends and family, especially at this season, but enjoying those meals is far more than sitting down at table. It's certainly not a fast food meal. It's a wonderful, slow experience that teaches us much about our loving God.

First, there is anticipation, not just of the food, but also of the friends who will enjoy it with us. We anticipate the flavors, savoring them in our imaginations, remembering nostalgically the last time we enjoyed them. We think about who could enjoy the meal with us and even anticipate the wonderful process of preparing the meal.

Next, we prepare. There is a lot to it. If we are really on top of our game, it begins with planting the right vegetables in spring. Top of Tom's list is heirloom tomatoes for his famous bacon, lettuce, and tomato sandwiches—a good, rustic sourdough bread, lean bacon with cheese melted over it, thick slices of tomato straight from the vine, sweet onion, avocado, and mustard or mayo, depending on taste. For our vegetarian friends, grilled squash, also fresh from the garden, replaces the bacon.

We recruit friends to help and then get to cooking. With much hilarity and fun, ingredients are diced and chopped. Fragrant aromas fill the house, tantalizing our taste buds. By the time we put the food on the table, our whole body is ready for the feast. We pile our plates with wonderful food, fill our glasses with the best of wine, and sit down with our guests and relish all that is set before us.

How do we prepare to taste the goodness of God? What seeds do we need to plant months in advance to enjoy the taste to its fullness? What tools do we need to help us prepare? Who do we invite to experience it with us?

> HOW DO WE PREPARE TO TASTE THE GOODNESS OF GOD? WHAT SEEDS DO WE NEED TO PLANT MONTHS IN ADVANCE TO ENJOY THE TASTE TO ITS FULLNESS?

A festive autumn meal is a wonderful, joyful experience in which we truly taste of the goodness of God. One church I know holds a harvest potluck each year at which only local produce is allowed. Tantalizing salads full of fresh squash, tomatoes, onions, and beans on a bed of local greens are everywhere. Chocolate zucchini bread and pumpkin pie tempt me. It is a wonderful way to taste and celebrate the goodness of God. In the United States and Canada, Thanksgiving coincides with this season, reminding us to be grateful for the abundance of God.

Last year when the autumn leaves were particularly vibrant with color and design, I designed a special exercise for our community as a fun way to mark the changing seasons and our gratitude toward God.

I collected a bunch of leaves of different shapes, sizes, and colors from the neighborhood, downloaded painted leaf patterns from Pinterest for inspiration, and we set to work. One person drew concentric circles on her leaves, expressing her desire to become more centered over the coming months. Another copied some of the colorful patterns I downloaded, finding relaxation and rest in the calm of the exercise. Another drew a picture of hopes for their family on one side of a leaf and of desires for their ministry on the other. I painted along the leaf skeletons, some with lines, others with dots, feeling as I did so that my hopes and expectations for the coming season are not fully formed.

At the end we coated our leaves with a water-based sealant, allowed them to dry, and then pressed them under a book for several days. I decorated our dining room table with my leaves, my first preparation for Thanksgiving over a month away. Tom and I continued to gather leaves on our daily walks and delighted in this ongoing reminder of the changing season and our need to continue thinking about hopes and expectations for the future. It was inspiring, reminding me that I am connected at all seasons to the earth and the God who created me.

PRACTICE
Have Fun with Leaves

We don't need to wait for autumn to paint leaves. It is always inspirational. Gather your journals, some colored markers or paint pens, and a Bible. Grab a picnic lunch and let's go look at leaves.

Plan a trip. Plan a trip to a place where you know there will be a variety of trees with different shaped and sized leaves.

Walk around the area. Walk around the area you have chosen. Take some deep breaths in and out to savor the fragrance of the tree-scented air. Invite the Spirit of God to calm your soul, and center yourself on the presence of God in all you see around you.

Look at the trees. Look at the trees and their different leaves. What shapes and colors catch your attention? Examine the leaves from several trees.

Pick the leaves. Pick the leaves that most appeal to you either from the tree (being careful not to damage the tree itself) or from the ground. Choose a variety of shapes, sizes, and colors. What is it about these leaves that you appreciate?

Find a comfortable place to sit. Sit in a comfortable place and thank God for the beauty of the trees you have seen and the leaves you have collected.

Arrange your leaves in front of you. Arrange your leaves in front of you and examine them. Trace their outline with your finger. Think about why you chose these particular leaves. How would you describe your leaves—strong, fragile, thin, unique? Write down the thoughts that come to mind as you examine them.

Read Scripture. Read through Ecclesiastes 8:1-15. As you contemplate the changing seasons your leaf collection represents, what thoughts come to mind? Perhaps you too are in a season of change. What is God saying to you about this change? Write down your thoughts. Are there key words you wrote down that could contribute to the design on your leaves? Are there emotions you would like to see expressed during this season, or ideas you would like to see fulfilled? Write these down and prayerfully consider how you could incorporate them into your leaf art.

Decorate your leaves. Decorate your leaves with different colors and designs. Trace along the skeleton and border of the leaf. Draw concentric circles to center your thoughts or create a free-flowing artistic design based on your meditation. When finished, pause, read through Ecclesiastes 8:1-15 again and write down what you feel you have learned about God and creation.

Display your artwork. Spread your art throughout the house. When you get home, press the leaves you have decorated between the pages of a heavy book for a few days, coat them a water-based sealant, and use them to decorate your house.

Make a leaf rubbing in your journal. To create a more permanent record make a leaf rubbing as well as (or instead of) coloring the leaves. Choose the next blank page in your journal. Place a leaf under it and gently rub over the skeleton of the leaf. Decorate the page with words and designs.

Reflect. Over the next week, take a few minutes each day to express your discoveries through a prayer to God. Write these in your journal or write a poem, draw a sketch, or even compose a tune.

HAVE SOME FUN WITH FRIENDS

This is a great exercise for a gathering of friends or a small group. Plan a trip together to a park or forest. Take a picnic lunch, your journals, colored markers, and Bibles.

Encourage each person to go out and use the preceding reflective exercise to guide them in an appreciation of God, creation, and rhythms of life. Over lunch talk about your experiences. What did you learn about God and God's intended rhythms for your life? What changes would you like to make to schedule as a result?

REST IN THE MOMENT

Let us sit in this moment
of God's creating.
Rest in its uniqueness;
savor its potential.
It is pregnant
with new possibilities
waiting to be born,
God's secrets not yet heard,
God's dreams not yet seen,
God's visions not yet realized.
Let us sit and look and listen.
Breathe in the fragrance
of its unfolding.
Stand in awe at its beauty.
Rejoice in its complex patterns.
Let us sit and imagine
new ideas waiting
for creative expression.
And join God in the creating.

In Denver a couple of years ago I was given a photo made completely of the words *Rest in the Moment*. I think the artist knew I was a master at worry and anxiety. Her image inspired me to relax and reimagine my life.

The previous couple of months had been tough. The property owned by our nonprofit organization Mustard Seed Associates had been vandalized, and our building destroyed. I felt God's presence embracing and comforting me, but I still struggled with questions of *what if*, *when*, and *how*.

At the same time, arthritis in my foot threatened to strip me of two of my greatest pleasures—walking and gardening. I was distressed over the past and afraid of the future. Yet hidden in the moment were some wonderful blessings that my fears and worries masked. Friends responded with concern, prayer, and wonderful suggestions of how to cope with my fears.

I washed some of the broken glass from the vandalized building, poured it into a large glass vase with a smaller vase in the center. Inside I placed a candle that when lit shone through the broken glass. It glowed with all the colors of the rainbow. Interspersed were patches of dark where leaves and dirt still remained. Everything else dropped away, and I was able to sit in the joy and sadness of that moment.

I was uplifted. Focusing on the moment, I enjoyed its gifts without worrying about the future or stressing over the past. After all, I couldn't change the past and I had no idea what the future would hold.

When I open myself to the Holy Spirit in this way, I am discovering, my anxious stuff gently washes away and I am left with a strong knowing of Christ my light, shining through my brokenness. Thankfully, I follow a "man of sorrows" who understands every shattered fragment of my life and is able to use those broken pieces to reflect his love into the lives of others in ways that are beyond me.

Children have a wonderful capacity to live in the moment like this.

"What did you do today? Who did you play with? Did you have fun?" Parents ask them every day after kindergarten or school, with the same puzzling responses.

"I don't know."

"I can't remember."

"I'm not sure."

Sometimes they honestly don't remember what happened an hour ago. The moment they skip out of kindergarten and into your arms, they have left school for the day and slipped into the present moment with you. They are genuinely not withholding anything; they have simply moved on and into the next moment when they can fully enter the joy of being with you again.

To rest in the moment that exists now, to relish the delight of its uniqueness and the gifts it brings to our lives like kids do, isn't easy. To find our contentment in God and fully savor the depth of godly revelation this precious, never-to-be-repeated moment holds, we must learn to let go of the past and be content in the present, no matter what our circumstances.

Paul's words in Philippians come to mind:

I have learned how to be content with whatever I have. I know how to live on almost nothing or with everything. I have learned the secret of living in every situation, whether it is with a full stomach or empty, with plenty or little. For I can do everything through Christ, who gives me strength. (Philippians 4:11-13 NLT)

I love reflecting on this kind of Scripture, especially in the framework of my daily life. It often inspires prayer or poems inviting me to pause for restful moments throughout the day.

Sometimes it is letting go of things that we love to do or people we care about. It could be letting go of hopes for the future or just of busyness and our fast-paced lifestyles. *, addictions ?*

So often we excuse our busyness by saying, "But I enjoy what I do." Yes, but does God enjoy it when it turns us away from the divine presence? We will never learn to rest fully in God unless we can relinquish our desire to be in control of our lives, our time schedules, and our activities, and do what we want to do rather than what God wants us to do. What distracts you from the divine presence and prevents you from fully appreciating the revelation of God in this never-to-be-repeated moment?

As I think of what it means to rest in each moment, I am reminded of Ann Voskamp's words in her inspirational book *One Thousand Gifts*:

> WHAT DISTRACTS YOU FROM THE DIVINE PRESENCE AND PREVENTS YOU FROM FULLY APPRECIATING THE REVELATION OF GOD IN THIS NEVER-TO-BE-REPEATED MOMENT?

"Life is so urgent it necessitates living slow." She is right. "In Christ urgent *means* slow."[1] Life is too important to be consumed in a blur of activity, too precious to not take notice of the God moments, the God love that bursts out in an unexpected hugs and unanticipated beauty.

How many God moments do we miss because we love to move fast, map out our lives, and be in control of everything that happens in our day? Then we get sick, lose our job, or have an accident. We lose control, and in grasping to secure the reins of our lives again we find we can never put them back together as they were before. We get angry, blame God, long for what was, and become resentful. Sound familiar? I think this was what the children of Israel wandering in the desert were experts at. They longed for the "comforts" of Egypt and in the process missed the God moments—the wonder of the desert with its harsh beauty and amazing miracles of God's daily provision.

BREATHING ROOM FOR THE SOUL

My recent research on rest and Sabbath provided important insights for me as I grappled with how to rest in the moment. Comparing different translations on BibleGateway, I looked up several psalms that talk about resting in God. Rest, from a biblical perspective, is definitely not about taking a nap when we are exhausted or relaxing in preparation for a busy week ahead.

In Psalm 62:1-2, one of my favorite verses on rest, *The Message* talks about "breathing room for my soul." What a beautiful way to describe the rest we find when we wait quietly and allow the presence of God to fill us. "Breathing room for the soul": that wonderful place of intimacy where we delight in God and God delights in us.

Rest like this does not just happen. Breathing-room moments are created by intentionally pushing aside our worries, sitting quietly, and imagining God in us and around us, filling us to overflowing with the wonder of a warm embrace. They are brief, personal, deliberate pauses in our busy schedules that allow a sense of stillness to dissipate the concerns of the day.

"Isn't this is what we call mindfulness?" you might ask. Of course the answer is yes. All faith traditions and even the secular world accept the need to mindfully pause and rest in the moment—God moments of delight, savored, relished, and enjoyed.

We talk about it all the time, yet it is still hard to do. We get busy or distracted. We forget what is really important. Yet we still believe that restful pauses throughout the day matter. Even my Fitbit tells me to relax for a couple of minutes every hour and encourages me to get up and walk regularly. In fact, I have learned to use these walking breaks to relax not only my body but my soul and spirit. Sometimes I do a breathing exercise, make a cup of coffee, or walk into the garden for a breath of fresh air. There are lots of ways recommended by the experts to help us relax.

One challenge I faced in creating restful pauses throughout the day was that I misunderstood the concept of stillness, and I suspect others do too. Stillness does not always mean motionless. It is more of an inner than an outer discipline, an exercise in learning to pay attention to the *now* rather than the *was* or the *will be*. I can be still in my spirit while walking as well as sitting. I can find inner rest while knitting or gardening or painting.

Learning to rest in the moment and find breathing room for our souls is a powerful spiritual tool that does not require special space, special skills, or special devices to make it happen. We can all find stillness and enter into the presence of God a hundred times a day.

Here are some thoughts on how to accomplish this.

Press the pause button. Cultivating restful moments is a deliberate action. First, we need to notice and seek out the spaces that encourage rest. This might be a place in nature such as a waterfall or garden corner, or a special place at home such as a comfortable armchair, or even a local coffee shop, a park bench, or a space on our work desk where we invite God's presence. It can even be a relational space such as a cozy meal with friends or sitting with our kids on our laps. Noticing these places and visiting them regularly throughout the day is a wonderful way to experience breathing room for the soul.

Breathe deeply for a minute or two. Seek out one of these spaces. Sit comfortably with your feet firmly on the ground. Close your eyes. Take a few deep breaths slowly in and out. As you breathe in, be conscious of your breath passing in through your mouth or nose, filling your lungs with life-giving oxygen.

Hold your breath for ten seconds, then slowly breathe out, allowing the toxins in your body to be expelled. Imagine the tension, anxieties, and pressure in your body flowing out as you do so. Come to rest, calm your mind, relax your body.

Recite a breathing prayer and sit or stand quietly for a minute in the presence of God. Do this several times a day and it will improve not only your emotional health but your physical health too.

My favorite breathing prayer is this one I wrote several years ago, and I still often use it both for personal times and in seminars.

Breathe in the breath of God
Breathe out your cares and concerns
Breathe in the love of God
Breathe out your doubts and despairs
Breathe in the life of God

Breathe out your fears and frustrations
We sit quietly before the One who gives life and love to all creation
We sit in awe of the One who formed us in our mother's womb
We sit at peace surrounded by the One who fills every fibre of
our being
Breathe in the breath of God
Breathe out your tensions and turmoil
Breathe in the love of God
Breathe out your haste and hurry
Breathe in the life of God
Breathe out your work and worry
We sit quietly before the One who gives life and love to all creation
We sit in awe of the One who formed us in our mother's wombs
We sit at peace surrounded by the One who fills every fibre of
our being[2]

Notice the sensory experiences that allow your soul to breathe. As you
sit in your space, what catches your attention? Looking at or holding
an object, real or imagined, may enhance your ability to focus. Running
our fingers over a treasured photograph, a pocket cross, even a pebble
or seashell enables us to relax as it stirs memories of happy or meaningful times. I love to hold my mother's opal necklace in my hand. It
is an increasingly special object that connects me to beautiful memories of her love.

Sounds like water cascading over rocks, bells ringing, or birds
singing can also help relax us. Pause and listen to the sounds around
you. Focus on one you have not paid attention to before, for example,
passing traffic or colleagues talking. Listen to birdsong or footsteps on
the path outside. Get lost in the sound and allow it to take you on a
journey. If you are listening to the traffic, imagine the journeys that
drivers are on. Ponder where they have come from and where they are
going. Thank God for their lives. If you are focused on people talking,

don't listen to the conversation but to the music of the sounds. Allow it to resonate through your body. Thank God for your ears that can hear.

Perhaps it is not sounds but aroma—baking bread, freshly brewed coffee, the fragrance of flowers—that makes you want to pause. Maybe it is the texture of wood or velvet or a loved one's face that draws you into God's rest. It can even be the taste of a good meal or a piece of chocolate.

I love a suggestion my friend Tom Balke gave to heighten our awareness of these stimuli. He keeps a small box and squares of paper on his desk and writes down fragrances, sights, and sounds that hold his attention and make him pause. He places them in the box and opens it once a month, reliving the experiences and the senses he experienced.

What types of sensory stimuli allow your soul to breathe and enter the rest of God? Make a list and think about how you could use these throughout the day to find those restful moments your body and spirit crave.

Notice the beauty of God's world. Look out the window or go outside for a few minutes and focus on a natural object. Look at it as if you are seeing it for the first time. It might be a cloud, a flower, or an insect. Examine the details. Imagine the energy of God flowing into its creation. Think about its purpose in the world. Thank God for its creation. (If you don't have a window to look out, carry a small natural object like a pebble in your pocket.)

Take a moment to appreciate what you are doing. Pause occasionally in the midst of your daily activity to appreciate your work. Sit at the computer and look at your hands and thank God for the dexterity that makes your work possible. Think of your brain and thank God for your intellect, which facilitates your exploration and understanding. Look at the words you have written and thank God for language to express yourself with. Consider setting your phone to provide a reminder.

Recognize the actions that encourage rest and delight in God. Moses took off his shoes when he realized he had entered a holy place, and without his sandals on it was obvious that he was there to stay awhile. Lighting the candle in the midst of my broken glass created a similar breathing-room moment for me.

Kneeling or raising our hands in the air carries many of us into that place of rest. For others it is reciting a breathing prayer or walking the labyrinth. Or it might be coloring images, painting pictures and words on rocks. Playing a musical instrument, working on a jigsaw puzzle, weeding the garden—anything that relaxes you can provide a restful moment. Or perhaps it is writing a song or knitting or whittling. Sometimes it is in community—preparing a meal, singing, or gardening together are all actions I find can draw me into that restful presence of God. Even washing the dishes or vacuuming the floor are special, sacramental actions that can invite us to the place where we delight in God.

Choose your favorite creative activity (there are infinite possibilities) and contemplate how to incorporate a few minutes of this activity into your daily or weekly routine.

Writing breathing prayers and garden walks are both helpful actions for me. The following prayer has provided a particularly good focus over the last few months.

God, I rest in this moment of your creating.
I breathe in the essence of who you are.
I breathe in your love of laughter and fun.
I breathe in your delight at creativity and diversity.
I breathe in your faithfulness to justice and freedom.
I breathe in your grief at pain and suffering.
I breathe in your joy at generosity and caring.
God, I rest in this moment of your creating
And find breathing room for my soul.[3]

Imagine yourself entering the place where God waits. I love to imagine God waits in my heart for me to enter the inner place of quietness where my soul and spirit are in sync with *the rhythm of God's eternal breath.* I found this phrase in Irish poet John O'Donahue's poem "In Praise of Air," which he wrote not long before he died, and it continues to resonate in my soul.[4] When I enter that place where my soul is in rhythm with eternal breath, I often spontaneously clasp my hands, close my eyes, and bow my head. It may only last for a few seconds, but in that brief moment there is a deep and profound connection to the living God.

Read a psalm or prayer. Use your favorite Bible app or create a file to bookmark your favorite psalms for easy access. Psalm 23 is probably the most popular for this, but others are equally enriching.

Practice gratitude. Pause for a moment as though frozen in time and look around at what you are doing and what makes it possible. What are three things you don't usually notice that you are grateful for? Is it the pens you write with, the electricity that powers your computer, or the windows that give you light? Sit in the presence of these things, express your gratitude to God for their creators and those that maintain them. Give thanks to God for your ability to use them and the creativity they enable you to express.

Contemplate what inspires you. Writing down and meditating on what I hear God say in these quiet moments is one of my most profound spiritual experiences. It keeps me grounded in my faith and inspired in my work. It is here that I often write the prayers I share on my blog (godspacelight.com) or start new creative practices for the coming seasons. For example, John O'Donahue's words "May our souls stay in rhythm with eternal breath" inspired this prayer/poem as well as the epigraph of chapter five. Their words resonate in my soul even more deeply than his original words.

> May our hearts beat
> to the rhythm of eternal breath,

our spirits be filled
with the wonder of eternal presence,
our lives embrace
the joy of eternal love.
May we know the Eternal
in us, around us,
before us, behind us,
and welcome the triune God
in every thought and word and deed.[5]

My prayers crafted during these moments often become the focus for future God moments of stillness and contemplation. I don't expect this but when prayers come, they are a gift that I receive with gratitude and continue to thank God for as I use and reuse them.

Reflect at the end of the day. Take a couple of minutes at the end of each day to reflect on what you have done and how it has affected you and your relationship to God. Write a sentence or two in your journal, draw a sketch, or highlight a few bullet points. Put the day to rest and relax.

Revisit the exercise at the end of chapter one, or ask yourself, *What gave me joy today?* and *What quenched my joy?* Follow this with *What could I do to increase my joy?* Imago Dei Christian Community has adapted Ignatius of Loyola's prayer of examen into what they call an awareness examen that is another great resource for this.[6]

Now, you might like to pause and create your own breathing-room moment. Sit quietly with your eyes closed and your hands clasped gently in your lap for a few minutes. Contemplate the suggestions in the previous paragraphs. Read the

> WHERE HAVE YOU CLOUDED YOUR ENJOYMENT OF GOD IN THIS PRESENT MOMENT BY SUCCUMBING TO THE WORRIES OF THE PAST OR ANXIETIES FOR THE FUTURE?

prayers. Savor the wonder of God's warm embrace. Look around you. What catches your attention? What fears and worries distract you from being fully attentive to God in this moment? What resentments and frustrations surface? Where have you clouded your enjoyment of God in this present moment by succumbing to the worries of the past or anxieties for the future? How is God asking you to respond?

CIRCLING PRAYERS

One form of prayer that I find particularly helpful in encouraging me to pause and rest in the moment is circling prayers, which were widely used by Celtic Christians in the fourth through eighth centuries. Circles were very significant to the Celts, and it is not surprising that circling prayers or CAIM became an important part of their prayer life.

The Celtic cross, composed of a circle superimposed on a cross, expresses the unique way Celtic Christianity incorporated the people's sense of wholeness in creation and joined it with the image of Christ. The Celts often transformed pagan symbols, recreating them as Christ-based practices. The circle was a pagan sign depicting the sun or the earth, the natural world. By superimposing it on the cross, the Celts expressed their view that the revelation of God comes to us through the natural world and in the person of Jesus Christ. We need both to get the full picture, so the two are bound together with the circle at the intersection of the natural and the spiritual realms.[7] This calls me to recognize the image of God in all persons and the presence of God in all creation.

It was felt that a circle with no break was a complete whole affording no access to the devil. Monasteries were often surrounded by a circle of crosses declaring that the space within was sacred and different— dedicated to God and claimed as a place where God met people who were offered sanctuary and hospitality.

A typical CAIM visualizes what we want God to keep in the circle of our lives and what we want to resist and keep out.

In times of danger, the inhabitants of the Outer Hebrides would draw a circle round themselves and their loved ones. Using the index finger of the right hand, they would point and turn round sun-wise reciting a prayer such as:

The Sacred Three
My fortress be
Encircling me
Come and be round
My hearth and my home.[8]

At other times an actual circle path was created around a room, a building, or community, as the Celtic monks did with their monastic circle of crosses. Circling prayers can then be recited as people walk a mini-pilgrimage around the area. They can also be used for house blessings, protection, and spiritual strength.[9]

I have been inspired by this concept and started writing my own circling prayers about ten years ago. Here is my first effort at such a prayer:

Circle us, Lord,
Keep love within, keep hatred out.
Keep joy within, keep fear without.
Keep peace within, keep worry out.
Keep light within, keep darkness out.
Stand in the circle with us today.[10]

At a recent workshop one participant, a teacher who was concerned at the growing violence in her school and neighborhood, decided to get her students to write words of peace and hope on stones. Her intent was to circle the school with these stones as a protecting circle around the facility. I hope she has been able to do this.

Another fun possibility is to look for circles in nature to inspire your prayers. They are everywhere. From the smallest grain of sand, which is worn by the sea into a circular shape, to the sun and moon that dominate our skies, from our fingers and the rings that encircle them to the spiral patterns in leaves or a special rock, and of course the mysterious crop circles—all are circles. When you find one, pause and say a circling prayer. Create a beautiful God moment for yourself.

I love that some circles are perfect, some form spirals, some are broken, distorted, disfigured, or scarred. Yet in all, the circle pattern is discernible. As we notice these circles, we can rejoice with God and the promise of wholeness and completion that the circle offers us. We rejoice too with those who have borne witness to this dream of wholeness throughout the centuries, living their lives to bring healing, freedom, and abundance to the oppressed, the hurting, and the abandoned.

I have been inspired by rainbows, curling bark on trees, and spiral patterns in shells. I use them to write circling prayers and for restful pauses. The following prayer was inspired by watching a double rainbow one afternoon. I snapped a picture, wrote the prayer on the image of the rainbow, and printed it out as a card to keep with me during the day. It still prompts me to pray, reminding me to keep looking, listening, and noticing all that is around me in each moment of the day.

God, circle what is good within me.
Nourish it,
Grow it.
Christ, circle what is true within me.
Awaken it,
Free it.
Spirit, circle what is holy within me.
Cherish it,
Sanctify it.
Righteous and faithful God,
Circle your image within me.
Give it life.[11]

PRACTICE
Walking in Circles

This circling-prayer exercise is adapted from a traditional CAIM. Use it to focus your attention on the moment. Pause for a couple of minutes or use it as a more relaxed, longer exercise to focus your day or even for a season of your life.

Sit with your eyes closed. Take a few deep breaths in and out. Imagine the circle of God's presence surrounding you. Recite the words "Circle me, Lord" several times and allow your spirit to rest.

Draw a circle. Extend the forefinger of your right hand and draw an imaginary circle around where you are sitting. Envision God enfolding you in a cloak, and ask God for peace to hear the divine voice. Repeat the words "Circle me, Lord."

Imagine Christ. Imagine Christ with his arms outstretched as on the cross, binding together the elements of the natural world and the built world of your dwelling into a sacred circle of wholeness. What stirs in your mind as you do this?

Open your eyes. Open your eyes and draw a circle in your journal or on a piece of paper to represent the encircling presence of God. If you have time, go for a walk and gather small rocks. When you get home lay them around your circle. Add the words "Circle us, Lord." What is embraced by the circle of God's wholeness for you? Where in this moment are you aware of God's wholeness and the completion of the healing both of creation and of all humankind that the circle represents?

Contemplate your circle. Remind yourself of the attributes of God you want the circle of your life to embrace in this moment and in the place where you sit. Write them around the inside of the circle and envision that enfolding cloak of God around you.

What do you want to keep outside the circle? Outside your circle write the emotions and feelings you want to be excluded from God's enfolding cloak. Are any of these currently inside your circle but need to be pushed out?

Who stands within the circle with you? Do your family and friends stand with you in the circle? Do your colleagues and workmates? What about the homeless and dispossessed, the hungry and unjustly treated? Write their names in the circle you have drawn.

Who stands outside the circle? Should they be brought inside? Perhaps you feel distanced from a colleague or your spouse. Perhaps you are suffering from compassion fatigue. What could you do to bring others into the loving circle of God's embrace? Write these names outside your circle.

How is God's creation bound with us within that circle? God's loving circle doesn't only encompass people, it encompasses the creation too. What of God's creation does your circle presently encompass? What does it exclude? Write down what comes to mind.

Write your own circling prayer. As a response to this exercise write your own circling prayer. Use this template: "Lord, circle me, keep . . . within and . . . without." Read through your prayer. What other inspiration comes as you meditate on it?

HAVE SOME FUN WITH FRIENDS

Gather with your friends or small group. Take time for each person to perform the "Walking in Circles" exercise on their own.

Stand together in a circle holding hands. Have each person in turn walk around the group reciting a circling prayer, either one that came out of the exercise or the "circle what is good within me" prayer, substituting *us* for *me*.

Before you disband your circle, discuss your responses to the circling prayers that were said over you. What further action does this prompt you to initiate?

CULTIVATE GRATITUDE

Thank you, Lord,
for your faithfulness in the morning
and your comfort at night.
Thank you, Lord,
for love that never gives up
and forgiveness
that never says no.
Thank you, Lord,
for mercy and freedom and life.
Thank you, Lord,
for companions on the journey, for burdens shared,
and caring shown.
Thank you, Lord, for you.

The week before the US Thanksgiving is my gratitude week. There is no equivalent in Australia to this wonderful celebration, and I have embraced it with great enthusiasm. I don't just relish the food, the friends, and the fun it brings together, but also its important reminder to give thanks for all the blessings of my life.

I begin each day by asking, *What are three things I am grateful for today?* Then I ask *What would my life be like without these blessings?* A loving husband, a beautiful garden, and good friends around the world immediately spring to mind. Without them I would be lonely,

1st world privilege

depressed, and unsatisfied. As the week progresses I am reminded of things I take for granted—flush toilets, warm showers, electricity. Without them my life would be harsh, unsanitary, and uncomfortable. I am so grateful for all the blessings of my life. Joy wells up inside me; I want to dance and sing around the house.

Unfortunately, I find that unless I make this intentional commitment to practice gratitude, it never happens. Gratitude doesn't come easily for us. In her fascinating book *The Gratitude Diaries: How a Year Looking on the Bright Side Can Transform Your Life*, Janice Kaplan comments on a survey she conducted for the John Templeton Foundation that showed "most of us suffer from a huge gratitude gap. We know we should be grateful, but something holds us back."[1]

She provocatively suggests, "We understand there is something that makes us more fulfilled—but we don't jump to try it? It's as if there were a magical happiness rock sitting in the middle of a field and half of us didn't even bother to go over and pick it up."[2]

naive

What would our lives look like if all the complaints, frustration, anxiety, distrust, confusion, criticizing, and grumbling were swallowed up in a life of thanksgiving?

"Grateful people reframe whatever happens to them. They don't focus on what they're lacking; they make sure they see the good in what they have,"[3] says Kaplan. When I read those words, an Australian classic, *A Fortunate Life*, by Albert Facey came to mind. I read it as a teenager and have never forgotten its powerful message. It chronicles his extraor-

> WHAT WOULD OUR LIVES LOOK LIKE IF ALL THE COMPLAINTS, FRUSTRATION, ANXIETY, DISTRUST, CONFUSION, CRITICIZING, AND GRUMBLING WERE SWALLOWED UP IN A LIFE OF THANKSGIVING?

dinary life of hardship, loss, friendship, and love. Documenting his early abuse and poverty, the horrors of World War I, wounding at Gallipoli, and his return to civilian life, Facey's story would leave many of us bitter and resentful. Yet Facey always believed he was a fortunate person. Every woe was worthy of praise and gratitude.

Gratitude is about changing our perspectives, not our circumstances. We can all reframe what happens to us with gratitude, not resentment, recognizing the richness of our lives in comparison to others. I am grateful for flush toilets, but millions in our world don't have them. It is an added delight to think about how I could I make someone else's life better by making this luxury available to them.

So why don't we grow up grateful?

In *Unless You Become Like This Child*, theologian Hans Urs von Balthasar helps us understand. He suggests that gratitude is resident in our hearts from our conception but needs to be brought to the surface. "In everything the human child is dependent on free acts of giving by others: in him, plea and thanks are still indistinguishably one. Because he is needy he is also thankful in his deepest being before making any free, moral decision to be so."[4] As we express gratitude, we become more grateful and start to realize that all we have is indeed a gift from God. "Only the Christian religion, which in its essence is communicated by the eternal child of God, keeps alive in its believers the lifelong awareness of their being children, and therefore of having to ask and give thanks for things. Jesus does not insist on this childlike 'say please,' say 'thank you,' because otherwise the fits would be refused, but in order that they may be recognized as gifts."[5]

The benefits of gratitude are huge, from greater life satisfaction and self-esteem to happiness, hope, empathy, and optimism. Gratitude changes entitlement into appreciation. It improves our relationships and helps us recognize our interdependence, encouraging us to treat others with respect. It is, I suspect, part of the essence of who God has created us to be.

Matthew Fox expresses some of this same sentiment in his insightful book *Creativity*. He sees gratitude as "the ultimate enabler. It moves us from apparent laziness to heroic giving. It can move mountains. That is why gratitude is the ultimate prayer."[6]

not always Gratitude is the ultimate enabler. Yes, yes, and yes! Gratitude enables those struggling with depression to break out of their despondency. It empowers those who feel hard done by to count their blessings. It encourages all of us to appreciate what we have rather than constantly wanting more.

IN ALL THINGS GIVE THANKS

Old Testament Israelites were predominantly a thanksgiving people. They didn't just thank God for the abundance and blessing of creation but also for their liberation from Egypt and all the gifts of life they enjoyed. The psalms in particular are alive with expressions of gratitude and thanksgiving toward God.

In the New Testament, Jesus infuses life with this same enthusiastic thanksgiving toward God. When he raises Lazarus from the dead (John 11:38-44) and when he transforms loaves and fishes into a feast for thousands (Matthew 15:29-38), he gives thanks. He thanks God for revealing the kingdom to the childlike and encourages those he healed to thank God for their restoration.

Most profound of all, at the Last Supper, Jesus gives thanks for the wine and the bread before it is consumed. The word *thanks* throughout the New Testament is the Greek word *eucharisteo*—which gives us Eucharist, another name for Communion. Each time we take Communion, which is modeled on this last feast Jesus enjoys with his friends, and stand with our friends and fellow worshipers before the Lord's Table, it is an act of pure thanksgiving. No wonder this central sacrament of our faith is sometimes called the Great Thanksgiving. This is the place where all followers of Jesus are invited to gather and share fellowship with each other as we remember and respond to the Eternal One who gave everything to draw us back into the embrace of divine love.

The great thanksgiving—but what am I grateful for as I partake? To be honest this is the first time I have really asked myself this question. As I thought about it today, a great list came together and my joy overflowed.

1. I am grateful for Christ, who came in the flesh to show us the face of a God of love and compassion and generosity.

2. I am grateful for the sacrifices Jesus willingly made, allowing his body to be broken and his blood to be shed so that we could be set free.

3. I am grateful for all who take Communion and partake of the Eucharist together, not just in my congregation but across the world—people from every tribe and nation and culture, male and female, rich and poor, disabled and whole, well thought of and despised.

4. I am grateful for those who have gone before, leaving footprints for me to follow that challenge me to a deeper level of action for justice, healing, love, and compassion.

5. I am grateful for those who will come after and continue the healing work that God has begun.

6. I am grateful for the bread and the wine, for the earth that grew the flour and grapes, for the human hands that shaped them, and for those who distribute them.

7. I am grateful for the God who reached into the soil of the earth and molded it into beings responsible to steward and look after this earth.

8. I am grateful that each human being is infused with part of the essence and image of God. This we see now in part but one day will see it emerge in its fullness, brought to wholeness through the work of the renewing and restoring spirit of God who lives within all of us.

Paul carried this same attitude of gratitude with him in his luggage when he traveled, and he encouraged his followers to do the same. His letters are full of gratitude for friends, for supporters, for spiritual gifts, and for growth in his disciples. He recognizes too that when we focus on the positive, praying with thanksgiving, our anxieties and worries lift and our lives and faith become stronger (Philippians 4:6).

Gratitude is meant to be central to our faith and spiritual practices. It's time to set it back where it belongs.

JOY-SPOT SIGHTINGS

Sue Duby, a colleague of mine on board the mercy ship MV *Anastasis*, told me she was most content when her heart felt like it was smiling with gratitude, when her "God lenses" peered out, making her aware of God's presence. One of her students coped with sadness, grief, and rough days by noticing the things in her day that made her smile. She called them "joy spots." Sue and her husband, Chuck, accepted the challenge and began to call out to each other "There's a joy spot" when something made them smile too.

As time progressed, this became a practice of naming things each day they were grateful for. Sue said, "The discipline worked a new muscle, but over time, it became a natural part of our day. We found ourselves not only 'naming' thankfulness in the morning, but actually looking for things to add to our list during the day. Our hearts smiled. We grew expectant."[7]

Then, one day as she read Philippians 4:6, "Do not be anxious about anything, but in every situation, by prayer and petition, with thanksgiving, present your requests to God" (NIV), she decided that every time she asked God for something, prayed for someone, or expressed fear, she would force herself to stop and be present to God in that moment. Then she named something related to her request that she was truly grateful for—before asking God for anything. A sense of peace and calm followed. Now, she says, the prayer often seems secondary, the need less urgent, and the sense of God whispering "I've got it covered" more clear.[8]

I love this practice. It encouraged me to also notice, name, and journal about my own joy spots of gratitude.

There are many ways that don't take a lot of time to incorporate joy spot sightings into our lives and our faith. Consider setting aside a few minutes on the way to work, while folding the laundry, or cooking to try some of the following suggestions. Or incorporate them in your family spiritual disciplines. Many websites give lists of suggestions on how to become more grateful, but the following list adapted from the Edison Township School District newsletter is what I have found most helpful.[9]

Make a vow to count your blessings. "Research shows that making an oath to perform a behavior increases the likelihood that the action will be executed. Therefore, write your own gratitude vow, which could be as simple as 'I vow to count my blessings each day,' and post it somewhere where you will be reminded of it every day."[10]

Keep a gratitude jar. Pause at the end of the day to ask, *What am I grateful for today?* A gratitude jar on your desk with some small slips of paper, like my friend Tom Balke has, helps. Write your joy-spot sighting on a piece of paper and add it to the jar. At the end of the week, read through the joy spots, reminding yourself of all you have to be grateful for. Identify the three things you are most grateful for. Write them in your journal. Focusing on the good in our lives changes our attitude, transforming challenging situations into positive feelings.

Be grateful for people. Gratitude toward people energizes us more than gratitude for things. Sundays are gratitude days for Tom and me. We often talk about what we are grateful for in each other. It is an invaluable spiritual exercise that highlights everything from how we make each other laugh to how passionate we are about the injustices in our world.

When we tell people why we care about them and what we appreciate in them, we boost their self-respect and dignity. We show them we love them not because of how they dress or what they have but because of who they are. In the process we often spark moments of joy for all of us.

One fun way to express this is by making gratitude rolls, a suggestion I came across on the blog *How Does She?* Get everyone in your family, home group, or friendship circle to write down something they are grateful for. Print these gratitudes out on small pieces of paper and bake them in rolls for a special thanksgiving meal. Crescent rolls are ideal for this because the small pieces of paper can be rolled into the crescents. I love the author's suggestion that we make a game of it. Get the recipient to read out the thanksgiving, and then everyone tries to guess who wrote it.[11]

Shower friends and family with joy spots, not stuff. Impulse buying diminishes how we value our possessions. Encourage recycling or reusing items that give joy rather than giving new stuff. There are lots of creative ways to do this: One possibility is a fashion show where you tell stories about your favorite clothing items and then give them away or swap with a friend. Another is a recycling party where everyone brings items they want to see transformed and reused, and shares the story of the item and why they want to reuse it.

I have long wanted to do this with the sweaters I have knitted over the last thirty years. I can't bear to throw some of them out because of the joy-filled memories they stir. Sharing their stories with friends and families would, I think, not only fill my gratitude cup but also enable me to let go and willingly repurpose them.

Write thank you notes. I love getting thank you notes in the mail but rarely write them. Unfortunately, it seems to be a thing of the past, yet it's actually a perfect way to express gratitude. Start a new discipline for the month. Write one gratitude note each day to a friend, family member, even a shop assistant or person who has been particularly helpful.

As an author I know how much I appreciate notes from readers that tell me what they enjoyed about my books, but these are rare. Teachers, doctors, helpful librarians, waiters in restaurants, family friends, and even neighbors whose gardens we admire all appreciate our grateful thanks.

Keep a gratitude journal. A gratitude journal is probably the most popular way to express gratitude. I do this on Sundays as part of my weekly journaling practice. You too might like to set aside time regularly to recall events or people you are grateful for. Take time to savor and relish the memory of what comes to mind. View it as a gift. Write about it and embellish your writing with happy faces.

Surprisingly, according to psychologist Sonja Lyubomirsky, a weekly journaling practice is probably better than a daily one to record what we are grateful for.[12] This was a relief to me. I found trying to keep track every day was not only overwhelming but also became a little contrived and my joy level soon diminished. That is how gratitude became part of my Sunday discipline. Journaling my gratitudes has helped me negotiate many storms and focus on the hope and joy of the life I am privileged to live rather than my fears or feelings of failure. Expressing gratitude has changed me dramatically, both making me more aware of the love of others and empowering me to express love for them. How do we express gratitude and learn to focus on the joys and not the fears in our lives?

> HOW DO WE EXPRESS GRATITUDE AND LEARN TO FOCUS ON THE JOYS AND NOT THE FEARS IN OUR LIVES?

Link your gratitude to thankfulness to God. What impressed me about Sue and Chuck Duby's practice is they linked their gratitude to thankfulness to God. They were aware that the joy spots they identified represented God's blessings on their lives and the situations they were concerned about. Spirituality and gratitude go hand in hand. Reading through the gratitude psalms or creating a gratitude prayer of your own is one good way to accomplish this.

My thanksgiving prayers often remind me of the contrast between the world as it is and world God is bringing into being, and they encourage me to respond to the needs I see around me. Here is one I wrote a couple of years ago that does this.

Thank you, Lord,
that in a world filled with hatred,
we worship a God of love;
in a world overrun by violence,
we believe in a God of peace;
in a world consumed by despair,
we embrace a God of hope.
Thank you, Lord,
that in a world afraid of scarcity,
we follow a God of abundance;
in a world full of abuse,
we trust in a God of justice.
Thank you, Lord,
for your presence in us and around us,
for all you are and will always be,
for all you call us to be.
Thank you, Lord, for you.[13]

At other times, my prayers express what I need to thank God for, as in the following prayer, which I wrote at the end of autumn as a reminder of the changing seasons and the variety of thanksgivings that each season reminded me of.

God, we thank you for blessings,
for the bounty of summer harvests and the beauty of creation,
for sunshine, light, and warmth,
for fun and laughter and fellowship with companions on the journey.
God, we thank you for blessings,

for the joy of the long days of summer
and the delight of even longer friendships,
for the brokenness in my soul
that is falling away like autumn leaves,
for the resilience growing within
to be stored for the dark days of winter.
Now, Lord, as the length of day fades
into the approaching night,
let me too find balance
and the grace to slow when I need rest.
Nourish and grow the light stored within me.
May it carry us through seasons
of outer darkness.
Plant that which has died
and use it to create new life
as we await the rebirth of spring.[14]

Regularly revisiting and reciting prayers like this adds to my list of thanksgivings in special ways. Sometimes I rewrite the prayer in my journal, highlighting the words that stand out for me, sketching responses and new thanksgivings along the sides. It is an enriching and delightful exercise.

Share your blessings. The old saying "It's better to give than to receive" has stuck around for a reason, the same reason that movies like *Pay It Forward* are popular. It really does feel good to help someone else even when it involves sacrifice on our part. Look for opportunities to help others and get your kids out there doing the same. Welcome new neighbors with homemade gifts or with the offer of tools they may not have acquired yet.

When our next-door neighbors moved out recently, they gave us their lawn mower, which we were then able to share with the new neighbors. We were grateful, and so were they.

Find ways for your kids to help too. What is one thing they are grateful for that could be shared with others? Maybe they have clothes they have loved but grown out of that could be donated to a local thrift store. Or maybe it is a favorite toy from past years that could be given to kids in a homeless shelter. Sharing like this makes kids place greater value on what they have. They are less likely to take their blessings for granted.

Be optimistic. We all see the glass half-empty sometimes. When you feel like griping at someone, look for that joy spot that unveils the brighter side and slip it into your gratitude jar. Guided gratitude interventions like this are one technique used with patients who have suffered traumatic, life-changing injuries.[15] As individuals practice and embrace gratitude, they are able to adjust, cope, and develop positive attitudes even in the most depressing situations. Wow! Imagine what a difference that would make to our lives.

Savor surprises. Unexpected or surprising events tend to elicit deeper levels of gratitude. Familiarity does breed contempt where gratitude is concerned. Documenting the surprises we are grateful for, like an unexpectedly beautiful sunset or a visit from a friend, should be at the top of our list.

Sometimes we need to look for these surprises. This morning, our first frosty morning of the year, as I walked around the backyard I was mesmerized by the unexpected surprise of ice crystals on leaves and wooden benches. The beauty of the patterns they created was breathtaking, yet I could so easily have missed them.

Awaken your senses. Our appreciation of the world comes through all of our senses. Touch, smell, sight, taste, hearing, and movement all wake us up to the incredible miracle of what it means to be alive. Noticing, savoring, and giving thanks for these gifts is a powerful practice. As you walk along the street and brush against your neighbor's garden, take notice of the fragrances that arise.

Use visual reminders. Visual reminders can serve as cues to trigger thoughts of gratitude.[16] As we race through life, we forget to be grateful. That is part of what I love about celebrating Thanksgiving. It is such a wonderful opportunity to bring together the people we love and are grateful for. Take photos, share stories, look intently into the eyes of those who gather. Store their faces in your memory and be grateful for them.

PRACTICE
Plan a Gratitude Scavenger Hunt

Playing thanksgiving games is a wonderful way to identify and show gratitude without being too serious. They bring positive feelings into our lives and relationships, and are exhilarating to play at home or at work. They are particularly helpful if you have trouble identifying what you are grateful for. So, go out and look for the things in your life that you are grateful for.

Get out your journal, and in large letters at the top of a page write "Ten things I am grateful for." You might like to spread this over several days—maybe work on one or two areas of gratitude each day. Get a stack of Post-it Notes and walk around your house identifying what you are grateful for. Use a different color for each gratitude you add and embellish your words with doodles or sketches. When you are finished, prayerfully ask yourself, *What would be different in my life without them?* What other gratitudes does this stir?

Use the following list to identify ten things you are grateful for.[1]

- Name someone who makes your life better. What about them are you grateful for? Write a thank you note in your journal, and at the first opportunity write it on a card and send it to them.

- What is something in nature that makes you smile? Take a photo or sketch it in your journal.

- Describe something that smells amazing. What comes to mind as you think of it? Write or draw the grateful memory it evokes.

- What is something that tastes good that you are grateful for? Write it in your journal, then take a taste break and sample it.

- What or who makes you want to laugh? What do you enjoy about that thing or person? How could you express your gratitude?

- Think of something you used today that you normally take for granted but now are grateful for. Write it down, draw a picture, take a photo, or go out and use the item.

- What is one thing in your life you are grateful for that you would like to share with someone else? Write down what you plan to do to accomplish this.

- What is one thing you have done in your life that you are particularly proud of? Write it down and why you are grateful for this opportunity. Is there someone you want to share this thankfulness with?

- Write down one thing you have learned recently that you are particularly grateful for.

- Describe a challenging experience in your life that you are grateful for. Why? How could you represent this in your journal?

Once you finish your list there are several possible ways to use it.

- Find some magazines and photos. Cut out images that represent what you have written in your journal. Create a collage from the images.

- Write the key words from your gratitude list on small pieces of different colored paper, cut them into shapes, and create a wreath. Or cut them into squares and create a gratitude quilt.

- Take thank you notes to the people on your list.

- Plan a party and celebrate the people, smells, tastes, and sounds you are grateful for.

- Write a prayer of gratitude and read it each day over the following week.

HAVE SOME FUN WITH FRIENDS

Plan a special thanksgiving meal together. Get each person to complete the "Gratitude Scavenger Hunt" before you gather.

At the meal share your gratitude list.

Go around the table and share what you are grateful for in each person present.

Last, express your gratitude to God for the many blessings in your life.

SEE THINGS DIFFERENTLY

Listen, as an act of love,
to the stories
of ordinary people
in everyday life.
Open yourself
to hear from joy-bringers,
love-givers, pain-endurers,
all the unsung heroes
who fill our world.
Take time to hear the wisdom,
find the wonder,
allow the poetry to emerge.
Let us look, listen, and proclaim:
People matter.
We care.
God loves.
All lives are extraordinary.

A couple of months ago a friend sent me a link to a delightful video in which a kid is paired with a friend and asked, "What makes you two different from each other?" Their answers are completely different from what any adult might think.

To our adult eyes, each kid looks very different from their friend. Some are Caucasian, some Asian, some Afro-Caribbean. Different skin and hair color: some healthy and athletic, some in wheelchairs. Their replies have nothing to do with wheelchairs, race, or hair, however. "She never stops talking!" says one white boy of his Asian friend. "I have smaller toes than Artie," says another active child of her wheelchair-bound companion. "I like gymnastics, and she likes swimming," says a fair-haired child of her dark, frizzy-haired friend. The best of all is the two little boys the video cuts back and forth to. One is Indian, the other Caucasian, though they are dressed in matching school uniforms. They look at each other in puzzlement and finally with many sighs and nervous glances, decide they like different games best. The caption at the end of the entertaining and thought-provoking video sums it up perfectly: "When it comes to difference, children see things differently."[1]

It's not just when they look at each other that kids see differently. The whole world is painted with a different brush for them. It's not a bed but a trampoline. A box is transformed into a train. Dad is really a superhero.

Kids don't worry about what others think, either, and are not afraid to spend all their time doing what they enjoy rather than what others think they should do. No rules tell kids they can't wear one bright blue and one pink sock together. Nor are there restrictions on painting trees purple or red. If that's what they like, that's what they do. And their feet will dance to the rhythm of their choices. Most importantly, they are unafraid to let the world see their joy and happiness; in fact, they want to share them with everyone.

Jesus saw people and things differently from us too. Take Jesus' view of the woman who anointed his head with expensive perfume, for example.

Meanwhile, Jesus was in Bethany at the home of Simon, a man who had previously had leprosy. While he was eating, a woman came in with a beautiful alabaster jar of expensive perfume made from essence of nard. She broke open the jar and poured the perfume over his head.

Some of those at the table were indignant. "Why waste such expensive perfume?" they asked. "It could have been sold for a year's wages and the money given to the poor!" So they scolded her harshly.

But Jesus replied, "Leave her alone. Why criticize her for doing such a good thing to me? You will always have the poor among you, and you can help them whenever you want to. But you will not always have me. She has done what she could and has anointed my body for burial ahead of time. I tell you the truth, wherever the Good News is preached throughout the world, this woman's deed will be remembered and discussed." (Mark 14:3-9 NLT)

Simon, presumably healed by Jesus, judges her with harsh criticism. He sees a woman not welcome in this gathering, forgetting that he himself was once unwelcome in the society that cast out lepers. Perhaps she was rejected because she made guests feel uncomfortable. After all, in this culture women did not eat with men. Plus the extravagance of her gift contrasts with their own lack of giving.

We judge her harshly too. To the disdain shown by those eating with Jesus, we add our own unseeing eyes of rejection. Is she a prostitute, as the account in Luke says? There has been much speculation over the centuries, but no one can be sure. We tend to assume the worst. She might have been Mary Magdalene, as John suggests. Perhaps she was someone else unacceptable within the society— maybe she was ill or poor or a Gentile. We don't know. We don't even know her name. What we do know is that Jesus saw not an outcast but a courageous woman coming into a place where she knew she would not be welcome. She came to share a lavish gift, a gift that Jesus sees for what it is: not as a waste of money but an outpouring of great love that anoints his body for burial.

Interestingly, this story occurs just a couple of days before the Last Supper, where Jesus washes his disciples' feet. I wondered as I read these two stories together recently, *Is this because this woman, like Jesus, challenges us to look with different eyes and think about all those we still exclude from our table fellowship?* In the story of the woman washing Jesus' feet, he embraced the outcasts and is eating at their table—the tax collectors and Simon the leper are there but are unwilling to welcome this woman. Jesus invites them to see her through different eyes and reach out to yet another outcast with appreciation for her great gift.

At the Last Supper, Jesus now invites his disciples to see him from a new perspective too. Perhaps, with the memory of that recent experience in their minds, he wants them to see him as he saw the woman. He too is rejected by society but welcomes them with open arms, pouring out a lavish gift, his life, for their anointing and cleansing. Maybe as he kneels, some of them are reminded of this woman and how they rejected her. Is she unnamed because she represents all the nameless and rejected ones in our society who we still refuse to welcome to our table and into our lives—people that we aren't willing to listen to because they are different from us or unacceptable in our own Christian culture? Or is it because in some ways she is the image of Jesus, anointing all of us for

> WHAT BIBLICAL STORIES DO YOU THINK YOU SHOULD REIMAGINE WITH CHILDLIKE VISION? WHAT DIFFERENCE MIGHT IT MAKE TO YOUR FAITH?

the work of the kingdom but in the knowledge that we, like our Anointer, will be outcast.

I know this is all speculation, but reading this and other Gospel stories with the awe and wonder of fresh and different eyes is part of what grows and strengthens our faith and makes our hearts rejoice. It all brings us back to Luke 10:21. God's ways are indeed revealed not through the eyes of the wise and the intellectual but through those of little children.

What biblical stories do you think you should reimagine with childlike vision? What difference might it make to your faith? *lazy!*

SEEKING NEW LANDSCAPES

The French novelist Marcel Proust once said, "The real voyage of discovery consists not in seeking new landscapes, but in having new eyes."[3] We can travel the world and keep our eyes closed to the newness emerging around us, or we can engage in every new experience as an opportunity to expand our spiritual vision and improve our eyesight.

For example, when Tom and I went to Australia for Christmas, it wasn't just the trip that refreshed my eyesight, it was rethinking my devotional time for the journey. I usually convert my office into a sacred space at the end of November with candles, prayers, and inspirational icons or photos. At the center is an Advent garden, a small contemplative garden with plants and candles, my replacement for an Advent wreath. Obviously, I couldn't pack this in my luggage, and the Australian agricultural department would have confiscated my garden anyway. *How do I bring joy to God while I am away and capture God moments with fresh eyes*, I wondered? Just getting ready for the trip pushed me outside my comfort zones and prompted me to revitalize my spiritual practices.

With great delight, I realized that my primary spiritual practice would be enjoying my family. No pressure to do intense Scripture study. Just fun and thanking God for my brothers. We revisited all our childhood haunts and even drove past the house I grew up in. We shared meals and reminisced. These were special practices that brought joy to my heart, and I am sure delighted God too.

In the same fun-seeking spirit, I felt I needed a special but different journal for the trip, something that would encourage new creative exercises, provide fresh perspectives, and draw me into God's joy. I explored journal formats. There are a lot of them out there I discovered as I browsed Pinterest for inspirational ideas on art and bullet journaling. I even considered scrapbook and collage journaling as new ways to record my thoughts. I finally bought a notebook with blank parchment paper, which gave me more scope for creativity. I purchased colored gel pens and downloaded decorative fonts to print key words I wanted to meditate on during my trip.

Reimagining my spiritual practices for this trip forced me to see things differently. Not in words but in colors and designs. It was enriching but relaxing and highly enjoyable. It blew out the cobwebs and revitalized my spiritual life in ways I never expected.

Irish poet and author John O'Donohue explains,

When you regain a sense of your life as a journey of discovery you return to rhythm with yourself. When you take the time to travel with reverence, a richer life unfolds before you. Moments of beauty begin to braid your days. When your mind becomes more acquainted with reverence, the light, grace and elegance of beauty find you more frequently. When the destination becomes gracious, the journey becomes an adventure of beauty."[4]

My Australian trip felt like a reverential journey of discovery as I let go of my existing practices and allowed God's beauty to emerge. It was exhilarating and enriching.

To reshape our spiritual practices periodically, intentionally planning to give God delight and experience God's delight in us is awe inspiring. Trips away, life transitions, seasons of the year, or the Christian calendar all provide fantastic opportunities to create new and appropriate transformative spiritual practices that draw us closer to God and into the beauty and joy of intimacy. Asking that question, What would I enjoy doing that will bring joy to God's heart during this season? has revolutionized my planning and my delight in God's presence.

My Advent gardens came out of this kind of questioning. I was bored with Advent wreaths and wanted something meaningful but fresh and new to focus on during the Advent season. For my first garden, I planted half a dozen succulents in a large basin. I painted rocks with the weekly themes of love, joy, peace, and hope on them and placed them around the plants. I pushed a candle into the soil near each rock and lit the appropriate candles each week. (The only problem was that some of the plants got a little singed.)

For a new mother, the most important spiritual practice could be delighting in her child and savoring God's joy in her newborn. My friend Ricci told me that after her son was born, her most spiritual moments each day were breastfeeding. Tragically, she felt guilty because she had no time to read the Bible or pray in the traditional ways. As we talked, however, she was able to see with fresh eyes, recognize God's delight in her and her infant, and rethink this as a spiritual practice of enjoying God.

For those who have recently moved into a new home, the enjoyment of settling into a new place and inviting God into that space could be an important spiritual focus. When we remodeled our house recently, I experienced some of this kind of joy. We celebrated afterward with a house-blessing party. I took some of the leftover broken pieces of tile from the kitchen counter and asked people to write words of blessing on them. People painted pictures, wrote lyrics and prayers, and decorated words and letters. I ended up with a bowl of special Scriptures, sketches, and blessings that now sits in our guest room for future visitors to add to. I loved it, our friends enjoyed it and I am convinced God delighted in it too. The memories of that evening, relived as I look through that bowl, bring yet another round of blessings with added joy and connectedness to God.

Spiritual practices are not set in concrete—"this is the way you must pray or read the Bible" type of patterns. They are more patterns of purpose than of form. If we ask ourselves, *How can I bring joy to God today?* we might come up with different perspectives and create something other than our usual singing a song or reciting a Bible verse.

The possibilities are limitless. I might find myself sitting in awe at a sunset splashed across the sky and give thanks to the Master Artist who created it. Or I notice the raindrops on a leaf and am awed by the light shining through them. On other occasions I watch kids on the swings in our backyard and feel God's love well up within me as I enter their exuberance and love of life. Enjoying life is an essential part of our connection to God; how we express it has almost infinite possibilities and will continue to change as we change and the culture around us changes.

BEYOND OUR CULTURE-BOUND VISION

The great British theologian, missionary, and author Lesslie Newbigin said, "The fact that Jesus is much more than, much greater than our culture-bound vision of him can only come home to us through the witness of those who see him through other eyes."[5] And in Revelation 7:9 we read, "I looked and saw a huge crowd of people, which no one could *even begin to* count, representing every nation and tribe, people and language, standing before the throne and before the Lamb, wearing white robes and waving palm branches."

People from every nation means many different perspectives. One entertaining way to expand our childlike vision and see Jesus and the Gospel stories with different eyes is by looking beyond our culture-bound images to the perspectives of that great crowd of people from every tribe and nation.

Leroy Barber, African American speaker, author, and founder of The Voices Project, has made me very aware of how white our images of Christ are.

Now I deliberately look for paintings that help me see our Savior from the perspectives of Africans, Asians, Native Americans, Hispanics, African Americans, and Polynesians. These viewpoints not only give me new eyes but enrich my faith and expand my understanding of God. I am particularly indebted to Matt Stone, an Australian blogger who gathers images of Christ from around the world for this purpose.[6] Browse through his gallery (curiouschristian.blog). What do you learn about Jesus? How do these images make you want to respond?

Some of my favorite paintings of Christ are by Chinese artist He Qi who escaped hard labor during the Chinese cultural revolution by painting pictures of Chairman Mao Zedong. He was inspired by a picture he found of the Madonna and Child by Renaissance artist Raphael and started painting copies of it at night. So began his own journey into Christian faith.[7] He has painted dozens of beautiful, vibrant images with fresh perspectives on the Gospel stories—everything from the conception to the crucifixion and resurrection. I love using them as a focus for contemplation or visio divina.

Jesus Mafa is another group that impresses me and encourages me to look at Jesus differently. In the 1970s, Mafa Christians in North Cameroon in Africa wanted pictures of the gospel from their own culture. With the help of French missionaries, they acted out Bible stories, photographed them, and enlisted French artists to create sketches. Village scenes are alive with kids playing, planting the first seeds of my reimagined Jesus with a crowd of kids always around him. More than six million copies have been distributed to date in eighty-three countries, making me aware that I am not the only one who has been enthralled by these images.[8]

Walk to the cross in other footsteps. Some of the most powerful cross-cultural Gospel paintings I have seen are created to help us understand Jesus' walk to the cross from different perspectives. Profound and sobering images of the stations of the cross highlight the pain of our world today.

Gwyneth Leech uses refugees from Iraq and Sudan as spectators.[9] Adolfo Pérez Esquivel draws from liberation theology for his paintings,[10] and Karel Stadnik in Prague uses contemporary images of human suffering to make the journey of Jesus more real.[11] These images deeply affect my own view of Jesus' journey and stir some of the creative ideas I express during Holy Week, like barbed-wire crosses and barefoot pilgrimages.

Listen to new music. It is not just the visual arts from other cultures but music too that helps us shape new joy-filled traditions that are satisfying and liberating. On his blog *Global Christian Worship*, Paul Neeley, professor at the Robert E. Webber Institute of Christian Worship, shares a rich array of resources that bring the story of Jesus to life, including fascinating examples of multicultural worship and music from around the world.[12] At Christmas I intentionally look for hymns, carols, and sacred music from other cultures to help me expand my vision of Christ. More than anything, I love to watch the YouTube videos of African musicians who don't just play but dance and sway to the rhythm of the beat.

What images, music, and traditions from other cultures have encouraged you to look at Jesus with fresh eyes and see the Gospel stories differently?

Ask your friends. One simple way to explore other traditions is to ask friends and colleagues from other cultures. When Anna Ranson asked her Facebook page about Advent and Christmas traditions, the response was phenomenal. She was inundated with a rich assortment of new ideas, some of which I would love to adapt for

> WHAT IMAGES, MUSIC, AND TRADITIONS FROM OTHER CULTURES HAVE ENCOURAGED YOU TO LOOK AT JESUS WITH FRESH EYES AND SEE THE GOSPEL STORIES DIFFERENTLY?

my own celebrations. One lovely idea was an Advent activity tree. Anna sat down with her family and asked what they would like to see happen during the Christmas season. They chose twenty-four of the ideas, wrote each idea on star-shaped paper pieces, laminated them, attached a ribbon, and hung them on a tree branch. Some involved baking, decorating the tree, and touring Christmas lights in the neighborhood, but others were outward focused, encouraging them as a family to reach out to others less able than themselves.

Read through her list of traditions on her website, The Imagination Tree.[13] Is there one that grabs your imagination? How could you adapt this tradition for your own use?

Go online. All cultures have unique traditions worth exploring and possibly adapting for our own use. Whychrismas.com is one of my favorites to browse through before Christmas.[14] My own Australian, Scottish, and Greek heritage has given me a love of Scottish shortbread, English fruitcake, and Greek baklava, which always feature prominently at our Christmas open house. However, my research has enriched these offerings with others, such as Austrian strudel, Norwegian cheese, Indian samosa, and Chinese dumplings.

One engaging French custom I discovered is where *santons* or "little saints" from the local village are placed in a traditional Nativity scene during Advent. The little saints come wearing their work clothes to visit the Holy Family. They bring the Christ child presents they have made or grown, hunted or sold. They offer simple gestures of thoughtfulness. The baker brings a special loaf marked with a cross baked only at Christmas time, the vegetable merchant, soap maker, cheese vendor, and wine grower bring their produce. The grandmother has knitted socks for baby Jesus, and a woman brings soup for Mary's recovery. A gypsy, often despised as a thief, brings her baby and a tambourine to sing to Jesus. A small boy brings only a bundle of sticks for a fire to keep the baby warm. A poor old man who thinks he has nothing to give the baby holds his lantern and offers to light the way for others. *Santons* come from all occupations, all classes of society, and all ages of people, and are represented. When we read about this tradition a few years ago, it inspired us to ask, Who do we welcome to the manger to share the good news? and provided the focus for all our Advent reflections.

Emma Morgan at Eastern Hills Community Church in Sydney, Australia, adapted this idea for her church. Each week during Advent, they focused on a different segment of society that would be represented around the manger. First, they invited those close to their hearts—family and friends. Week two they invited those who were close to their lives; week three those in the community who treat them with kindness and service; week four those who are abandoned, forgotten or not coping; week five, Christmas Day, they brought themselves and finally those who have shown us how to follow Jesus.[15] What a fun and fresh way to celebrate the birth of Christ.

Visit other churches. Not only can we be inspired by the traditions of other cultures, but other churches or denominations can help us think outside the box and inspire our creativity too.

Visit churches in your neighborhood and ask them how they celebrate Advent and Christmas, Lent and Easter. I am sure you will be inspired by their ideas and might even find some creative new practices for yourself. Or if you are visiting another country, make an effort to attend a church service in another language even if you don't speak it fluently.

In a similar vein, I love to collect crosses from different countries and faith perspectives. I have Ethiopian, Roman Catholic, Russian, and Greek Orthodox crosses; Jerusalem, Huguenot, and Celtic crosses; and many more. My collection expands yearly, enriching faith and appreciation of those who see Christ different from me.

For example, St. Georges's cross, immediately recognizable as the English national flag, I learned recently, would be better known as the Palestinian cross because St. George was from Palestine. As a conscript in the Roman army, he decided to stand up against the persecution of Christians in the fourth century because he was so disgusted by the barbaric methods employed by the empire. He was so impressed by the faith of those who died believing in Jesus that he became a Christian himself, even though he knew that this would mean certain death. St. George's Church at Lod, near Tel Aviv in Israel, is the alleged resting place for his body.

Richard the Lionheart adopted George as the English saint in the time of the crusades, probably because he was impressed by this hero who was beloved by Christians and Muslims alike. Among Palestinian Christians, St. George is known as a protector of the home, a healer, and someone who stood up against the misuse of power. What a beautiful story that helps me see Palestinian Christians differently while enriching my knowledge of Christian history.[16]

PRACTICE
Make a Rainbow

"I am the Light of the world," Jesus tells us in John 9:5. We imagine a bright, shining light, white and pure, but white light isn't really white at all. The unnoticed miracle of everyday light is exposed in the rainbow. Every rainbow is a revelation of the colors that dwell at the heart of white light.[1]

The light of Christ too is made up of all the colors of the rainbow, all the rich and varied hues of different cultures, tribes, and perspectives, as well as the different colors of creation that we have caught a glimpse of in this chapter.

Make a rainbow. Fill a large bowl or dish halfway with water and prop up a mirror inside it so that part of the mirror is under the water and part is out. Place the rainbow maker near a sunny window with direct light coming in so that it hits the mirror (early morning or early evening light works best).

Alternatively, use a bright light to shine on your rainbow maker.

Play around with holding a large white piece of paper above the maker to catch the rainbow. (You might have to move a bit until you find it.)

Move the paper closer to the mirror and then farther away to see how your rainbow changes![2]

What colors are revealed that you were not previously aware of?

What other colors do you think are still hidden from you?

Write down the impressions that come to mind.

Imagine the rainbow hues of the light of Christ. Do an internet search for rainbow images of Jesus from other cultures. Visit Global Worship and check out the Jesus Mafa images for Holy Week and He Qi's artwork, or look through the nativity scenes on worldnativity.com.[3]

Print out one image from Africa, Asia, South America, Polynesia, the Caribbean, and Australian aboriginal culture, and spend a few minutes meditating on them. Reread Lesslie Newbigin's words: "The fact that Jesus is much more than, much greater than our culture-bound vision of him can only come home to us through the witness of those who see him through other eyes."[4] How has your culture-bound vision of Jesus been changed by viewing your images?

Visualize the rainbow colors and different cultures that come together through these images to shine the full light of Christ in our world. What rainbow colors of Jesus are revealed that you were previously unaware of? What new perspectives do your images bring? Write down the impressions that come to mind.

What creativity does this exercise ignite within you, and how do you feel God prompting you to respond? Perhaps you would like to reimagine the story of Christ from another cultural perspective. Or you might like to experience Christ in other cultures by visiting churches that view Christ differently.

Write, draw, record, or create your response in whatever media you are inspired to use. Listen to music from other cultures while you work. If you are inclined, dance or sing in a way that you feel is appropriate for that culture.

HAVE SOME FUN WITH FRIENDS

If you are meeting as a group, get together for a potluck meal that celebrates the rich rainbow colors of Christ's light. Have each person bring a dish from a different culture to share.

Before the meal, check out the websites mentioned in this chapter and print out images of Jesus that catch your attention. Spread them out on the table. Read the Lesslie Newbigin quote and sit in quiet contemplation of the images for several minutes. Listen to music from other cultures while you contemplate and share.

What colors of Jesus are revealed through your eating and sharing of images that you were previously unaware of? How do these change your perspective of Christ and of God's kingdom?

STAY CLOSE TO THE CRACKS

Stay close to the cracks,
to the broken places
where people weep
and cry out in pain.
Stay close to the cracks
where God's tears fall
and God's wounds bleed
for love of us.
Stay close to the cracks
where light shines in
and grass pushes up
through concrete.
Stay close to the cracks
where weeping wounds
open unexpected doorways
to healing and wholeness and life.

We are born compassionate. It is a deeply rooted instinct expressed before a child is a year old.[1] Infants react to people in distress wanting to help. Their sympathy increases when they are unable to respond or if no one else responds. Young children also seem happier when giving away a treat than receiving it.

We've all seen this kind of compassion in kids we know. They burst into tears at the sight of starving children on TV or a homeless person on the street. They exasperate their parents by giving toys, lunch, or pocket money away.

Those of us who believe in a compassionate, caring, and loving God shouldn't be surprised. Compassion is in God's DNA. It is in ours too. We are created to be conduits of divine love, and as that love flows from us in compassion and kindness, we are changed and God's image is restored.

COMPASSION NEEDS NURTURE

A child is born with that divine spark of compassion, but to keep this spark alive and growing in a world that is often indifferent to pain and suffering, it needs nurture.

The three most important ways to nurture compassion are modeling, surrounding ourselves with people who regularly practice compassion and coming face-to-face with people who need our care. Without role models to guide us, face-to-face encounters to prompt us, and encouragement to reach out and be kind, the impulse shrivels and dies. In our overprotective society where we don't want our kids to fraternize with the "wrong crowd," adults often discourage children from being compassionate to outsiders, especially to those at the margins. They hasten this turning away by protecting their kids from exposure to pain and suffering. Unfortunately, we deaden their compassion and desire to be kind, especially to those outside their family or community.

Yet we need compassion for our own healing. My prayer at the beginning of this chapter was inspired by the song "Anthem" by Canadian songwriter and musician Leonard Cohen, who sings "There is a crack in everything / That's how the light gets in."[2] When God confronts us with situations that need our compassion, it is so light can shine into the darkness. It is in the cracks, the broken places of our lives and our world where violence flares and pain cries out, that healing can happen. When we respond to brokenness with compassion, we take the first step toward our own wholeness.

Light shines and water seeps into cracks. Seeds lodge, germinate, and take root in these same cracks. Then out of these cracks come green shoots reaching for the sky like rays of light shining out through the broken places. We look with awe at the strength, wisdom, endurance, and light that comes from those who are struggling.

Father Greg Boyle explains:

> Standing in the margins with the broken reminds us not of our own superiority but of our own brokenness. Awe is the great leveler. The embrace of our own suffering helps us to land on a spiritual intimacy with ourselves and others. For if we don't welcome our own wounds, we will be tempted to despise the wounded.[3]

I don't think anything rejoices the heart of God more than when we show compassion to the most vulnerable and neglected in our society. I imagine God doing a happy dance, a little like the children did when Jesus threw the moneylenders out of the temple.

My own healing has been closely tied to compassionate service to others too. Listening to news about refugees never prepared me for the horror of Khmer camps, a horror that returns as I watch the flood of refugees today too. Stories of torture and abuse that still bring tears to my eyes stirred compassion in my heart but also surfaced memories of my own abuse. Responding in compassion opened cracks where light could shine and my own healing began.

When I settled in the United States, it was easy to ignore these heart-wrenching situations. Fortunately, some of my friends continue to work more directly with the marginalized than I was able to. Friends like Rich and Cheryl Mackey, who after they left Mercy Ships started a ministry to young people in Juarez, Mexico. Their stories continue to inspire me and keep me close to the cracks in our society.

Modeling caring behavior, even in small, everyday ways like saying "please" and "thank you," helps others learn to be compassionate too. It demands a deliberate choice to be warmhearted rather than self-indulgent. I try to say thank you to everyone from shop attendants to waiters and endeavor to give other drivers the right of way, even when I am in a hurry. It isn't always easy, though, and I often mess up. Online shopping has somewhat derailed my face-to-face thank yous, and I am not sure how to change that. Yet these simple acts of kindness help us and our kids grow into generous, kindhearted people. What simple acts of kindness could you perform today to keep you close to the cracks in the social fabric of our society?

One time I visited patients in the MV *Anastasis* hospital, I found a gaggle of kids sitting on the floor. Battered and beloved toys that had obviously seen many years of hard play were changing hands. Four-and five-year-old crew children, their hearts stirred with compassion for kids they knew had nothing, brought their favorite toys and joyfully gave them away. As they grew older, I watched these kids join their parents in the clinics, not just playing but helping tend patients and participate in the caring work they saw modeled. They are adults now. Some are doctors, nurses, and aid workers, others run their own not-for-profit organizations to reach out to the marginalized. All of them have deeply compassionate and caring hearts.

> WHAT SIMPLE ACTS OF KINDNESS COULD YOU PERFORM TODAY TO KEEP YOU CLOSE TO THE CRACKS IN THE SOCIAL FABRIC OF OUR SOCIETY?

For example, Heidi Metz started IMANI a couple of years ago to focus on bringing financial services to the unbanked and underbanked. The organization provides a mobile payment system that makes it possible to offer low-cost services to the unbanked anywhere in the world. Heidi believes that one way to treat the causes of poverty is to provide banking facilities that eliminate banking fees, a huge barrier to progress.

Mariska Lako also followed the example of her parents in dedicating her life to caring for the most vulnerable. She worked as a doctor in Sierra Leone during the Ebola crisis, often putting her life at risk to help others less fortunate than herself.

Jesus is a superb model for how and why we should care for others. He planted seeds of compassion wherever he went.

As I read the stories of Jesus, I meet a compassionate man whose heart ached for lost sheep, prodigal sons and daughters, abused and abandoned travelers, poor widows and those who hungered or were broken in body or spirit. This heartache made him challenge society's indifferent and judgmental attitudes. He encouraged his disciples to share generously without expecting anything in return. He empowered them to heal those who were broken in body and spirit. He sat down for dinner with the outcasts as well as the wealthy. These were the signatures of his life and ministry.

At the beginning of Jesus' ministry he stands up in the temple and reads the prophet Isaiah's words:

The Spirit of the Lord the Eternal One is on Me.
Why? Because the Eternal designated Me
to be His representative to the poor, to preach good news to them.
He sent Me to tell those who are held captive that they can now be set free,
and to tell the blind that they can now see.
He sent Me to liberate those held down by oppression.
In short, the Spirit is upon Me to proclaim that now is the time;
this is the jubilee season of the Eternal One's grace.
(Luke 4:18-19 my paraphrase)

Then, when John asks for proof that Jesus is the Messiah, Jesus responds,

> Go and tell John what you've witnessed with your own eyes and
> ears: the blind are seeing again, the lame are walking again, the
> lepers are clean again, the deaf hear again, the dead live again,
> and good news is preached to the poor. (Luke 7:22)

In case you think this was only for Jesus himself to model, listen to
what he says to his disciples:

> If you want to be extraordinary—love your enemies! Do good
> *without restraint*! Lend *with abandon*! Don't expect anything in
> return! Then you'll receive the truly great reward—you will be
> children of the Most High—for God is kind [compassionate]
> to the ungrateful and those who are wicked. (Luke 6:35)

Oops! How can we ignore that? Jesus calls us to be extraordinary
people of compassion and caring. This is probably one of the reasons
the early church grew as quickly as it did. Disciples shared meals,
houses, and money with each other. They looked after the poor and
the sick when others abandoned them. As a result, the early Christian
author Tertullian imagined the pagans saying, "See how these
Christians love one another."[4]

Church history provides many other examples of caring followers
of Jesus. One of my favorites is fifth-century Irish saint Brigid of
Kildare. She was such a tenderhearted child that she often gave away
her parents' possessions to beggars. Her frustrated father decided to
sell her to the local king as a slave. When he went to negotiate the sale,
however, he made the mistake of leaving her outside with his favorite
sword. Brigid gave the sword to a beggar, which of course angered her
father even more. The watching king reputedly asks Brigid, "What will
you do if I bring you into my household?" Her response, "I will give
your goods away too." He diplomatically tells her father, "I think she
is too good for me," and sends her home. Brigid grew up to become a

famous abbess in the Celtic Church, never losing her compassionate heart. As abbess of Kildare monastery she often provided one thousand meals a day to passersby. She became a bright and compassionate light to the Irish.

Brigid believed that Christ often came to us in the guise of strangers, so every stranger should be treated as we would treat Christ. Tradition has it that when churning butter she would make thirteen portions—twelve in honor of the apostles, used by the community, and an extra one in honor of Christ. This was reserved for guests and the poor.

How would it change us and the ways we look at people and respond to their needs if we saw in them the face of Christ? I can imagine that our compassion would blossom in amazing ways just as Brigid's did.

Francis of Assisi is another who challenges me to stay close to the cracks in the social fabric of our world. He fled a life of privilege, gave away his wealth, lived among those at the margins, and encouraged others to do likewise. His advice and the joy-filled life of poverty and service he adopted as a result are just as important a model for us today as they were hundreds of years ago. I thank God for Brigid and Francis of Assisi. Their hearts ached for the poor and the dispossessed just as Jesus' did, and they shaped their lives and ministries around that concern.

In a recent article for the Melbourne paper *The Age*, my friend Evelyn Heard, who just retired as chaplain for the Melbourne Royal Children's Hospital, told the story of a Holocaust survivor who faked a lame leg so he wouldn't have to walk into the gas chamber. On three occasions a Nazi guard carried the young man toward the chamber, but each time turned and carried him back again. The human acts of touch and eye-to-eye contact softened the heart of this guard, who had already sent thousands to their deaths, and made him respond with compassion. Evelyn says,

> Our perspectives might be different if we took the time to personally enter the space of people whose destinies we debate:

sharing a meal with an Indigenous family to hear about the unique ongoing challenges they face; having a coffee with a homosexual friend; eating baklava with a woman wearing a hijab or burqa, or a Middle Eastern gentleman; taking the time to sit and listen to tales of torture and cry with refugees as they recount their life's journey to date.[5]

Evelyn's compassionate heart is shared by her daughter Rachel, who at fourteen started an organization called the Carasa Foundation, which works to free children from slavery and provide medication, hospital care, and education to ensure that the demand for slavery is reduced.[6]

I find that one good way to connect face-to-face with those who need our compassion is by getting to know strangers in our communities. We live in disconnected worlds with little motivation to engage strangers, even neighbors. Online shopping and banking, drive-through fast food, and commuter lifestyles provide few places for face-to-face meetings.

With this in mind, I avoid drive-through windows and deliberately go inside to meet the people who serve me. I also visit farmers' markets and artisan fairs. When we attended our local farmers' market for the first time last year, a large sign proclaimed "Be compassionate, our farmers have had a hard year." The weather fluctuations from sudden cold to hot had devastated crops and created severe hardships for many. If I only buy food from the supermarket I am oblivious to our farmers' hardship and grumble at the sudden rise in prices rather than expressing compassion and sympathy.

When we stay close to the cracks, when we come face-to-face with those who need our caring concern, listen to stories of those who have been abused, share a meal with a woman wearing a burqa, and make our hearts ache with the need to respond, that is where caring begins and compassion flourishes.

IT ISN'T AS HARD AS YOU THINK IT IS

Feeling overwhelmed or nervous about the cost of compassion? You shouldn't be. Showing kindness isn't as hard as you think. It is as simple as inviting a neighbor over for tea or coffee, or taking them a plate of Christmas goodies because we are concerned about them. When we offer to help weed a neighbor's garden, share the produce from our own gardens, take a homeless person to the local sandwich shop, or respond to crises like hurricanes with clothing and food, our kindness is a form of compassion.

The challenge is to make this a daily rather than an occasional practice. Where have you modeled kindness and compassion today? is an important question we should ask ourselves regularly, maybe as part of our daily spiritual practices.

> WHERE HAVE YOU MODELED KINDNESS AND COMPASSION TODAY?

Think globally. Most of us are aware that we live in a needy world. There are seventy million refugees and millions more displaced within their own countries as a result of hurricanes, earthquakes, and famine. Walls at the border to keep out those we don't want, abuse of women, violence against African Americans, Hispanics, Muslims, or those of different sexual persuasions all speak of huge cracks in our social fabric. They overwhelm us. No wonder we suffer from compassion fatigue and create emotional barriers to protect ourselves. *What should I do, will the little I am capable of make a difference?*

Kids never seem to ask these questions. They see a need and respond without thinking. They show mercy to beggars, neighbors, and crying friends. Maybe that is why the little boy gave his lunch to Jesus. Perhaps sympathy welled up within him for the hungry people around him. Maybe it was the compassion he had seen Jesus model. He didn't think about how little he had; he came face-to-face with a need and knew he had to do what he could.

Act locally. A couple of years ago I started noticing brightly painted rocks with words like *peace, love, kindness,* and *thank you* on them appearing round our neighborhood. Some remained for a day, others became permanent fixtures, shining points of color, reminders of our need to be kind and compassionate. This is the Kindness Rocks Project, started by Megan Murphy, a life coach from Massachusetts who used to wander the beach at Cape Cod looking for tiny treasures like sea glass, shells, and rocks.[7] One day she wrote messages with a permanent marker on some rocks and left them on the beach. When a friend told her that finding one of the rocks changed her day, Megan knew she had found a way to inspire and help others.

The Kindness Rocks Project now makes a huge impact in communities across the United States. Colorful rocks brighten the days of strangers, help both creators and finders relax, and bring joy to their communities. For some, the painting of rocks provides a pathway out of depression. For others, it adds meaning to life or connects to them to their communities. Knowing that something as simple as a colored rock can bring a smile to a stranger's face is an incentive that has inspired many to be kind and caring. The beautiful thing is that kids love it and anyone can do it.

More recently I discovered Compassion Games, "a community engagement experience that invites people around the world to challenge one another to promote acts of compassion that better our lives, our communities and all life on Earth."[8] The organization encourages people to do acts of kindness in their neighborhoods. Their motto is "Survival of the Kindest." They think that compassionate acts have a catalyzing effect, creating a chain reaction of acts of kindness. Participants encourage others to play and spread the game from person to person and community to community. What a wonderful project both for us as individuals and for our churches to get involved in.

The Kindness Rock Project and Compassion Games show me that we can have fun practicing compassion and kindness, move beyond compassion fatigue, and train ourselves to make this a way of life.

Evidently making it into a game with stakes, challenges, and rewards builds resilience in us.

Read Matthew 6:2-4:

> When you do something for someone else, don't call attention to yourself. You've seen them in action, I'm sure—"play actors" I call them—treating prayer meeting and street corner alike as a stage, acting compassionate as long as someone is watching, playing to the crowds. They get applause, true, but that's all they get. When you help someone out, don't think about how it looks. Just do it—quietly and unobtrusively. That is the way your God, who conceived you in love, working behind the scenes, helps you out. (*The Message*)

Consider ways that you could do some random acts of kindness. If you are looking for ideas, check out Brad Aronson's blog post "103 Random Acts of Kindness—Ideas to Inspire Kindness."[9]

Involvement in our local communities shouldn't close our eyes to global needs, however. Seattle is a hub of international relief organizations, but we don't need to live in a place like this to get involved. There are hundreds if not thousands of organizations that respond to global needs. The important thing is to choose a few that tug at your heart, get involved, and stick with it.

CROSSING THE STREET
WHEN THE LIGHT IS RED

Staying close to the cracks and recognizing Christ in those I meet has challenged me to rethink my life with compassion for strangers in mind. Seeing poverty and injustice as I worked in the refugee camps in Thailand and then in Africa was devastating. Driving down along the Mississippi River to New Orleans and passing through communities just as poor was horrifying. Coming to terms with the fact that my lifestyle contributed was a mind-blowing spiritual revelation, and at times I do feel as though I am trying to cross the street of our society while the light is red.

When I asked myself, *How do my lifestyle decisions contribute to the injustices that create poverty? How can I work for the wholeness and abundance of all God's people and especially those at the margins?* I knew I needed to repent and make some radical changes in order to be a truly compassionate person. When I added, *How can I help to transform the lives of those who seem to have no hope of enjoying the privileges I take for granted?* I had to rethink how I shop and what I buy.

> HOW DO MY LIFESTYLE DECISIONS CONTRIBUTE TO THE INJUSTICES THAT CREATE POVERTY?

Tom and I have made a number of lifestyle changes that encourage more ethical, compassionate living to help provide for some of those living at the margins. We buy fair trade shade-grown coffee from Camano Coffee Roasters, partly because of their partnership with Agros International, a Seattle-based Christian development agency that empowers poor communities in Central America. We also buy fair trade locally produced Theo's chocolate because I know that over two million children in West Africa are employed as slave labor to grow cacao. Most challenging of all, we have looked for socially responsible investing opportunities, hoping that our financial investments will also bring about environmental sustainability and social change. I increasingly see these decisions as spiritual practices that draw us closer to our neighbors and bring rejoicing to the heart of God.

It's not easy to always shop or live with the world in mind, and I still buy books from Amazon and look for bargains. However, I struggle because I know that my decisions have consequences for others. By ignoring the issues, I condone the injustices God's beloved children live under. I can buy cheap clothing because Chinese garment makers work long, hard hours for a pittance. I buy cheap food and enjoy cheap meals because many farm and restaurant workers do not receive a living wage.

More than anything the modeling of the friends around me has most challenged me to look at fair trade as part of my Christian practice.

For example, ethically produced clothing is a relatively small but growing area of concern I was made aware of by my former assistant Katie Metzger. Katie is a cofounder of Same Thread, a fair trade clothing company that has enabled women in Thailand to live sustainably without prostituting themselves. She told me, "No matter what, when you buy Fair Trade, it can deepen your love. Love for the planet, love for your fellow human beings, and love for beautiful craftsmanship. Money cannot buy you happiness, but when you buy Fair Trade, your money will serve other people and the planet with compassion. And that's as close to happiness as money can buy."[10]

Greg Valerio, who lives in Chichester, England, championed fair trade jewelry as a spiritual concern Christians should care passionately about. Mining gold, diamonds, and other gemstones often leaves indigenous people impoverished, slave laborers, and victims of war. In November 2017 as he watched Ugandans mine the first fair traded gold in Africa he exclaimed, "This is an answer to prayer, the prayers of men and women who in their poverty, their exploitation, their weakness and the marginalization of the post colonial African economic settlement cried out for help, recognizing that on their own they will not overcome the immensity of the unjust scales that are weighted against them."[11]

Greg has dedicated much of his life to this fight and educated me and many others in the process. He encourages British Christians to buy fair trade jewels and gold for engagement and wedding rings as part of their Christian responsibility. He saw the first fair trade gold spire erected on Chichester Cathedral and has seen the triumph of lives in Africa and Central America changed by fair trade advocacy. Prayer, he says, is the active ingredient that generates hope, growth, and ultimately new life.

I thank God for activist friends like this who challenge me to recognize the spirituality of making more substantial compassionate decisions that can have major consequences for our poorest neighbors.

PRACTICE
Shine Light in the Cracks

Cracks and potholes mar all the roads we travel on. Go outside and walk along your street. What cracks do you see? Hunt around until you find one big enough for the light to get in. What is growing in that crack as a result? Take a photo or draw a sketch.

We want to cover cracks: cracks in the pavement with new concrete, cracks in our lives with a façade of laughter or a semblance of respectability. Look for a crack that has been repaired. Was this successful? Has the crack started to reopen? Is there new greenery growing? Take another photo.

Look for a crack where life has flourished and grown. Perhaps it has been converted into a rain garden, like the cracks in the pavement in the parking lot of our local mall. Or self-seeded flowers may be growing. Take a third photo.

Now come inside to your favorite sacred space for a time of reflection. *Sit quietly allowing God's love to wash over you.* Read through the prayer at the beginning of the chapter and examine your photos. If possible, listen to Leonard Cohen's song "Anthem." What thoughts and images of cracks in the social fabric of our world come to mind?

What cracks break your heart? Reflect back on the news you heard this morning. Remind yourself of friends who are suffering and in pain. Write these in your journal for prayer.

How have you tried to ignore or cover these? Are there ways you respond, perhaps with an indifference that show these are festering? Perhaps there are things you need to confess or seek forgiveness for. Offer these up to God in prayer.

Are there ways you are already responding that give you joy and hope? Think of the light that is shining into your cracks. Are you aware of green shoots emerging from within your spirit toward the sun? How could you nurture their growth and help them to thrive? Write these down.

Who else is responding that you could join? What local organizations already respond to the needs that make your heart ache? Are there ways that you could get involved? What else might God be asking you to do in response to the cracks you are aware of?

HAVE SOME FUN WITH FRIENDS

Before you get together with friends, have each person in the group take the three photos suggested in "Shine Light in the Cracks"—one of a crack, one of a repaired crack, and one of a crack where life is emerging.

Pass the photos around and give each person the opportunity to share why they chose to photograph these particular cracks.

Discuss the photos you took. What cracks in your own lives did they bring to mind? How could the life revealed in these cracks be encouraged to grow and flourish?

Images of cracks, open, filled

How might our wounds or brokenness increase our joy?

COME TO THE TABLE

Come, Lord, welcome into my space.
Dispel the fears and anxiety.
Align my heart to yours.
Create within me a fitting place
for you to dwell.
Come, Lord, welcome into my home.
Break down the barriers.
Fill it with generosity and caring,
peace and hospitality.
Create within it a fitting place
for others to dwell.
Come, Lord, welcome into this world.
Embrace the unlovely,
share with the unfortunate,
Enjoy the beauty of sights and sounds and fragrances.
Create within it a fitting place for you and for all humanity
to dwell in unity.

Tom and I are hospitality people. We don't merely love to cook meals for friends; we also love to provide a place for travelers to stay.

On one occasion about five years ago there was a knock on our front door. When we opened it two young men confronted us.

Mormons, we thought. Then we realized they were too scruffily dressed. *Can we sleep in your backyard?* they asked. They had found our address on a website about intentional community and knew we sometimes offered hospitality to people passing through town.

No, we responded, *but we have a spare room in the basement. You're welcome to sleep there.* They had come from a community in San Francisco and hoped to head north into Canada to work in another but couldn't get visas.

Our two young friends slept in our basement for a few nights and then moved into our prayer tower, still hoping to get their visas. They stayed with us for a year, sleeping on the floor in this tiny room that looked out over the lake and usually provided a sacred space for Tom and me. We called them our angels unawares. They repainted the kitchen and living room, installed new toilets, and refinished our rather dilapidated dining-room table. They worked in the garden, prepared meals, and entered with zest into our community life. They were a God-sent blessing we could easily have missed.

On another occasion a family of four landed on our doorstep after the husband suffered a breakdown that made it impossible for him to work for six months. More recently we extended hospitality to a student who was living in his car. Others have come for a night or just for a meal. We have entertained people from around the world, listened to incredible stories, and connected to their triumphs and joy as well as their pain and suffering.

Entering into people's lives like this has made me more sensitive to other needs in our community. The young student who lived with us made me aware that he is one of many who sleep in their cars because they cannot afford rent. A survey done by the University of Chicago suggests that one in ten young adults go homeless. Many of them are students.[1]

"Isn't it risky?" we are often asked. Yes it is, but the benefits far outweigh the discomfort. "You cannot embrace Peter and John," I am sure Jesus would have said, "without also accepting Judas." I suspect that when he sat down for that last meal with his disciples, Jesus knew the potential for Judas's betrayal, but he still reached out to embrace him. I wonder if he hoped that through this gracious act of hospitality Judas would change his mind.

Hospitality is an amazing thing. It encourages us to open our homes and our hearts to get to know others in ways that can't happen in public places. There's a special intimacy in opening your home or being welcomed into someone else's.

In his book *Reaching Out: The Three Movements of the Spiritual Life*, renowned priest and teacher Henri Nouwen calls hospitality "the creation of a free and friendly space where we can reach out to strangers and invite them to become our friend."[2] He goes on to suggest that the most important guests, the most important strangers we get to entertain in our homes are our children. When they are born, we don't really understand who they are or who they will become. "They are guests we need to respond to, not possessions we are responsible for."[3]

What wonderful imagery this creates for me. I love kids and especially enjoy watching how a newborn baby can become the focus of attention for a roomful of adults. We receive this child without question. Whether we are the parent or not, we are eager to embrace the child with joy. Yes, the child is a stranger but a stranger that we desperately want to see become a friend. We delight in its newness and uniqueness as special gifts. We want to spend time getting to know the child, encouraging it to develop the gifts God has placed within it.

Maybe hospitality is about receiving every stranger in the same way we receive a child.

THE RADICAL HOSPITALITY OF GOD

The entire biblical story revolves around the radical hospitality of a God who comes to welcome us all home to the kingdom banquet like newborn infants welcomed into a hospitable home.

Hospitality in ancient Palestine was more than a courtesy extended to friends and travelers. It was how villages determined whether strangers were friends or enemies, a threat or an asset to the community. Extending hospitality by providing food, water, and shelter was a way to temporarily adopt strangers into the community and hopefully convert a potential threat into a friendly alliance. Sometimes oil was poured over the head of the stranger as a sign of welcome.

This might be what David referred to in Psalm 23:5:

You prepare a feast for me
in the presence of my enemies.
You honor me by anointing my head with oil.
My cup overflows with blessings. (NLT)

David is probably not talking here about God preparing a banquet for us to eat while our enemies with empty stomachs sit around drooling over the lavish food we are enjoying. This verse offers an invitation to sit down and enjoy a meal with strangers and those we perceive as a threat, an encouragement to seek for understanding and reconciliation rather than division and hatred. It is a good example for us in today's world where so many feel surrounded by enemies of race, creed, and political opinions.

In Jesus' day this same kind of radical hospitality was considered more than a commandment. It was a sacred obligation filled with the joy of serving both others and God. Those who did not extend hospitality to orphans, widows, and the homeless could be rejected. Like early monastics and Celtic Christians, Jews believed that sometimes in welcoming strangers they welcomed angels into their midst.

So many of the vivid images we have of Jesus revolve around meals, festivals, and radical hospitality. Jesus repeatedly demonstrated the joy of hospitality as he fed the crowds, sat down to eat with tax collectors, and shared a Passover meal with his disciples. He ate with friends and strangers, rich and poor alike. Sometimes it even seemed as though he invited himself over for dinner. He performed his first miracle at a wedding feast, not only joining in the celebration but making it more fun for people by turning water into wine.

Even after Jesus' death, he came back to share meals as a way to communicate his message of salvation and hope. One of my favorite Gospel stories is of the risen Christ preparing breakfast on the beach for his friends—not a lavish banquet for the neighborhood but an intimate act of hospitality for his closest companions.

What difference would it make in today's world if we looked at all strangers in the same way we look at a child—an unknown but welcome person we hope will become a friend in our home.

Stop and think for a moment. Pull out a photo of a child you love or of your own childhood and your journal to write down your responses.

Read Luke 9:48: "Whoever welcomes a little child in My name welcomes Me. And whoever welcomes Me welcomes the One who sent Me."

How did you respond to the last newborn child you were introduced to? What feelings and emotions welled up within you? How did you greet and welcome the child? What changes in behavior were you willing to make in order to get to understand this child, accommodate its needs, help it feel welcome in your home? What further responses did your meeting invite?

Now think about the last time you met a stranger—perhaps a homeless person on the street or a new member at your church. How did you respond to that person? In what ways did you welcome them as you would welcome a child? In what ways did you endeavor to turn this stranger into a friend?

Prayerfully consider your responses. Are there ways that God might be asking you to rethink your approach to the strangers in our midst?

CELEBRATING THE GREAT FEAST OF LIFE TOGETHER

My life and Tom's seem to revolve around food, not just eating it but also preparing it. Our basic rule is—if you're in the house at meal time, your welcome to eat with us. Sometimes these meals are spontaneous. Friends drop by unexpectedly or are working in our office or garden and we share garden salads, cheese plates, and bread. Other meals are planned well in advance, and Tom prepares tasty casseroles with rice and beans and cheese, or more lavish feasts with roast chicken and vegetables.

Recently we hosted a Greek feast for friends who had served with me in our early days on board the *Anastasis* in Greece. I made dolmades—vine leaves filled with rice cooked with tomatoes, pistachios, and raisins; and vegetarian Greek-style meatballs served with yogurt sauce. Others brought pita bread with hummus, baba ganoush, and olive tapenade; Greek salad with lettuce, olives, tomatoes, cucumber, onions. and feta cheese; and baklava for dessert.

Some of us had not seen each other for thirty years, but we were still friends. As we ate and shared memories of our lives together, I was struck by how much this must have resembled meals Jesus ate with his disciples and other friends—the tax collectors and prostitutes. The pita bread wasn't just an add-on to the meal but an integral part, just as bread was at all Middle Eastern meals. I was suddenly overwhelmed by the feeling that in eating together we had shared in the communion of Christ's body.

"Breaking bread together" is still a phrase we use for hospitality and informal gatherings. Today we probably don't literally break bread, but the term still symbolizes shared life, togetherness, and community. In his wonderful book *Food and Faith: A Theology of Eating*, Norman Wirzba says,

Eating is about extending hospitality and making room for others to find life by sharing in our own. . . . Eating is an invitation to enter into communion and be reconciled with each other. To eat with God at the table is to eat with the aim of healing and celebrating the memberships of creation. . . . Food is a gift to be gratefully received and generously shared.[4]

I wonder whether we limit the celebration of our faith when we take hospitality out of Communion and consume the bread and wine in a sterile environment that disconnects us from the enjoyment of God in the midst of everyday life.

The early church celebrated Communion as the great feast of life. They believed they sat down not just with each other but also with God, who gave this gift of life to them all. Christians throughout the ages have often shared agape meals, love feasts rich with hospitality and sharing, reminding guests that in sharing food, Christ was present in their midst. As they sat down together, the barriers between rich and poor, slave and free, male and female were dissolved. Sharing meals opened a doorway to the wonders of God's eternal world in which we will one day all feast together at the great banquet celebration of God.

> DO WE LIMIT THE CELEBRATION OF OUR FAITH WHEN WE TAKE HOSPITALITY OUT OF COMMUNION AND CONSUME THE BREAD AND WINE IN A STERILE ENVIRONMENT THAT DISCONNECTS US FROM THE ENJOYMENT OF GOD IN THE MIDST OF EVERYDAY LIFE?

I caught a glimpse of this type of hospitality during my *Anastasis* days. One meaningful celebration we held in each port was what we called a "highways and byways banquet." Crew members went out into the streets and invited passersby on board for a meal. As ports are often in the most disreputable parts of town, it was not unusual to have prostitutes, drug addicts, and homeless people join us. Many had never been invited into a home before. It broke down barriers and sometimes led to life transformations.

Much to my surprise, when I asked one of our Mustard Seed Associate interns what she enjoyed most about her summer with us, she responded, "Our meals together." This was where she felt Christ's presence most profoundly. No matter what we are doing, we drop our tools and eat together. We share our lives, our struggles, and our wonderful stories of how God is working in us and in our world. It is here that we learn to respond to each other with kindness and compassion.

There is no better place to learn to listen, not to the answers in our own heads but to the unsettling questions others ask, than when sitting relaxed and comfortable around the table sharing a meal. It is here in the intimacy of our own homes that we are challenged to take Jesus' radical call to hospitality seriously and reach out with love, not hate, seeking to build bridges, not walls, to embrace compassion, not conflict. Hospitality is about listening to the voice of God with compassion entering our world, and it is in the place of listening that change can begin for all of us.

We live in a world of great division where we all need to sit down over a meal, not just with friends but with those we disagree with and see as a threat.

As you think about this what comes to mind? What situations are you currently facing that might be defused by sitting around the table during the coming months and sharing a meal? Where have you seen God prepare a feast that has brought enemies together and overcome fears and disagreements? How could you prepare a meal "in the presence of your enemies" and offer open hospitality to those you disagree with?

WARM FOOD, FRIENDSHIP,
AND LAUGHTER

Many churches already take seriously this call to dinner hospitality and have discovered the joy of reaching out with growing compassion and caring into their communities as a result. "In 2009, Saint Lydia's, a Lutheran church in Brooklyn, New York, garnered national attention when it began holding weekly services over dinner. Longing to dispel feelings of isolation often reported among young New Yorkers, founder Emily Scott decided to model her service around the early church practice of having a meal together as Eucharist."[5] She felt the earliest gatherings of Christians described in Acts 2:46, "they broke bread in their homes and ate together with glad and sincere hearts" (NIV), and based on Jesus' Last Supper, were intended to be a model for how Christians worship together. This new way of doing church, which Saint Lydia calls a "dinner church," often brings strangers together. "Throughout the evening, they read Scripture, sing, and pray, but most importantly, they eat. Central to the process of eating is engaging in dialogue, providing space to respond to the Scripture or sermon."[6]

A similar movement sprang up out of the Assemblies of God church in Seattle, where "Community Dinners" grew as participants asked, "What would Christ be doing with his time if he actually lived in our neighborhood?"[7] As they shared food, friendship, and laughter with their neighbors, they discovered that many struggled to find housing and employment. Reaching out with meals soon became an endeavor to provide homes and jobs for those they ate with.

Potluck Church, associated with Disciples of Christ in Madisonville, Kentucky, conducts informal worship services around a potluck meal that culminates in Communion.[8] They read Scripture, ask challenging questions, share prayers, and support one another's ministries and callings into the community.

Our own church, Saint Andrew's Episcopal Church, hosts a Jubilee lunch each month to which all are invited. Most of the guests are people who live on the streets and love the offer of a regular meal with people who over the years have become friends. Some of them now come to church and attend other celebrations we host. The kindness of a shared meal has opened all of us to compassionate responses to the homeless that we may otherwise not have considered.

To me the ultimate place of hospitality is not the Last Supper but the manger, that place where we welcome Jesus, the newborn child, into our world and into our lives.

In *Jesus Through Middle Eastern Eyes*, Kenneth Bailey's imagery of Jesus born in the middle of a family home rather than a stable has captured my imagination, prompting me to ask, *Who is welcome at my manger?* Bailey explains that the Greek word (*katalyma*) translated as "inn" in Luke 2:7 does not mean a commercial building with rooms for travelers but a guest space in a village home. Most houses at that time consisted of two rooms—one for the family and one for guests. At night animals were brought into an area adjacent to the family room. He believes that Jesus is clearly welcomed into a family home. "The child was born, wrapped and (literally) 'put to bed' . . . in the living room in the manger that was either built into the floor or made of wood and moved into the family living space."[9]

The words from Luke 9:48 come back to my mind: "Whoever welcomes Me welcomes the One who sent Me." I wonder, *Who welcomed the baby Jesus, the most important child ever to be born into our world?*

According to Bailey, the first to welcome Jesus and offer hospitality were Joseph and Mary, their families, close friends, as well as the animals. Then came the shepherds. Despised and seen as unclean by their society, they are visited by angels and invited to come home to celebrate the child who will become the Messiah. That they were welcomed and not turned away from this home is remarkable. This is good news indeed for the outcast and the rejected.

Then the wise men come, according to Bailey, rich men on camels, probably from Arabia. Foreigners also not normally welcome in a

Jewish home. They come to a place of hospitality and welcome that has beckoned to them across the world. They come offering the hospitality of their expensive gifts. This too is remarkable and good news for people of all nations who long for a place to call home.

There are notable exceptions though. The ones who do not welcome Jesus are the religious and political leaders of the day. Power and wealth make them ignore the One who is born to be Savior of the world. I wonder if some of the villagers didn't welcome him either. For some of them, Jesus must always have been the illegitimate son of Mary.

Jesus' birth calls us toward a new and welcoming home, a hospitable place where we all feel safe and loved. There are family, friends, and animals gathered with us. There are special invitations by angels for the despised and rejected, and a star to guide the strangers and those who seem far off. The new family envisioned in the birth of Jesus is one that offers open hospitality. It is inclusive of all who accept God's invitation.

The question that stirs in my mind is, Who will we invite to welcome Jesus with us? Who do we invite to this celebration that may otherwise be ignored or excluded? Do we reach out to people from every tribe and nation and religion? Do we invite Ebola or cholera victims, people of Syria and Iraq, those who have been forced into prostitution, and those who have violated them

> WHO WILL WE INVITE TO WELCOME JESUS WITH US? WHO DO WE INVITE TO THIS CELEBRATION THAT MAY OTHERWISE BE IGNORED OR EXCLUDED?

there? What about prisoners or people of other sexual persuasions? Perhaps the homeless who find more and more cities shutting them out deserve a special invitation, just as the shepherds did. What about those we are estranged from? Do we think there is a place for everyone in God's welcoming home? If so how do we extend that invitation so that these people feel the warm welcoming hospitality of God?[10]

PRACTICE
Welcome to the Manger

Sit quietly in your sacred space. Take some deep breaths in and out. Close your eyes and imagine this new imagery of the birth of Christ. Visualize Christ born not in a smelly stable but in a comfortable home and surrounded by a loving family that has welcomed Mary and Joseph into their midst. Imagine the excitement and the joy.

Read Luke 9:48: "Whoever welcomes a little child in My name welcomes Me. And whoever welcomes Me welcomes the One who sent Me." Sit quietly and allow these words to sink into your heart.

Who do you think was present at Jesus birth? What kind of welcome did they give this child?

How do you think Joseph's and Mary's parents responded? What about the other guests? How do you think they welcomed this child?

Compose a story or draw a picture of this exciting event.

How would you welcome the shepherds? Reread Luke 9:48: "Whoever welcomes a little child in My name welcomes Me. And whoever welcomes Me welcomes the One who sent Me."

Now imagine the arrival of the shepherds—despised, outcast, unreliable. How would you respond to their arrival? What would you think when they told you they had been visited by angels? Would you welcome them in to see the baby Jesus?

Who are the despised and rejected in your society that might be knocking on the door asking for hospitality and welcome?

Reflect on your own response to them. Add another paragraph to your story about their visit.

Foreigners welcome. Read Luke 9:48. Now the wise men arrive. Rich and powerful but strangers, not people of your faith, maybe even priests of another religion. How would you welcome them into your home? What would you think when they told you about the star they had followed?

Who do you think they represent in our society today? Who have you rejected because they come from another place, another religion, or another world view?

Reflect on your response and write another paragraph for your story. *Welcome to God's family.* Read Luke 9:48 one more time.

In the birth of Jesus we see the radical hospitality of God. Animals, family, strangers, despised, and wealthy are all invited. Who stands around the manger with you today? Who are you still excluding? How would God ask you to respond?

HAVE SOME FUN WITH FRIENDS

Have each person do the "Welcome to the Manger" exercise before they come to the group meeting. Encourage them to bring photos of those they would like to see welcome Jesus with them.

Take a large piece of paper and draw a manger with the baby Jesus in it at the center. Draw a circle round it.

Discuss the story of Jesus' birth as it is told in this chapter. Allow each person time to express their responses to the story.

Now talk about the people you want to see gathered around the manger with you. Place the photos around the circle as you share.

Look at the photos closely. Who is still excluded? Who in your immediate family or our worldwide community are not present? What could you do to help include them?

Finish with a time of prayer for the strangers, the excluded, and vulnerable you have identified.

EMBRACE TRUST

Draw your circle, Lord,
around us like a cloak.
Circle us
with life and love and laughter.
Circle us
with light and joy and presence.
Circle us
with smiles and hugs and friendship.
Draw your circle, Lord,
Let it radiate light where there has been darkness.
Let it birth joy where there has been despair.
Let it preserve life where there has been death.
Draw your circle, Lord,
over all the creatures of your world.
Let it bring wholeness and peace and unity.

When I asked my Facebook friends what childlike attributes they thought made us fit for the kingdom of God, the most frequent response was *trust*.

Childlike trust is amazing. Infants are totally dependent on and trust in the one who conceived and sheltered them until their birth, on the one who feeds, nurtures, and loves them during those first years of life. "Catch me, Daddy," a young child cries as they launch off a wall assured of their father's ability and desire to protect them from a painful fall. "I'm hungry; I'm cold, Mommy," they whisper, confident that a meal will appear and a warm bed be provided.

Childlike trust is special. It isn't earned. It is instinctual. It is a deep and abiding belief in the provision of love and sustenance that mirrors the trust we are meant to have in our loving God, who promises to sustain and provide for us just as a parent does. That too, I am convinced, is something we are born with, an instinctual knowledge that God is trustworthy no matter what we do.

Unfortunately, by adulthood we think of trust more as something to be earned. Reliability means "Don't let me down, make my life better, make me happier, and I will trust you." God must earn our trust too. When the Eternal One says, "Trust me," we say, "Show me you are trustworthy by giving me a happier life with all the trimmings." To play deprivation, nature deficit, awe depletion, compassion fatigue, and imagination suppression we add trust distortion.

Why have we left it until last? Even more important, why is it so hard for us to trust that God is as loving and caring and able to provide as the parents we trusted as children? *(not always so)*

Relearning trust in God is, in many ways, the end game of our journey. The new practices we have established, the childlike qualities we have regained weave together to cement our trust in the loving God, who is at the center of the universe, in ways that nothing else does.

> WHY IS IT SO HARD FOR US TO TRUST THAT GOD IS AS LOVING AND CARING AND ABLE TO PROVIDE AS THE PARENTS WE TRUSTED AS CHILDREN?

When awe and wonder flame and curiosity ignites, when we are inspired by nature and learn to see things differently, trust is reborn. Gratitude, compassion, creativity, and the ability to live each moment to its fullest braid together into a thick cord of trust that can never be

a vague argument

broken. When I dig in the dirt, laugh with a friend, gasp in awe at a sunset, or sit quietly and enjoy the silence of God's embrace, the Spirit of God rises within me creating a beautiful tapestry of love and trust.

This type of <u>trust is part of our DNA</u>.

My own journey through writing this book has drawn me closer to God in many special ways.

I have given myself permission to play and enjoy God, and found childlike delight in painting rocks, creating meditation gardens, and walking round my finger labyrinth. I have relished our awe-and-wonder walks, not just opening my eyes to the beauty of God's creation as it is now, but anticipating the changing seasons and the new vistas that will inspire awe. I have renewed my passion for hospitality and compassion, reconnecting with friends and organizations from the past. I have also found joy in revisiting my story and highlighting the presence of God in my past. This has both instilled trust and faith.

Most precious of all, my office has become a sacred space with a ring of candles around it—what I call my circle of trust. Each morning I light my candles and swivel my chair around my circle. I start with the candle in front of my photos of my family and friends, reminding myself of their love and support throughout the years. Then I pray for them.

My next "station" is a selection of photos, rocks, shells, and other memorabilia from places that have become *thin spaces* for me—Church of the Good Shepherd in Lake Tekapo, New Zealand, Iona off the west coast of Scotland, a majestic blue gum tree in Australia, Mayne Island in Canada, where we often go with friends for retreat and refreshment, Camano Island just north of Seattle. The memories of how God has lovingly met me in these places fill my mind. Reminding myself of God's faithfulness in the past makes it easier to trust for the future.

From there my eyes move to contemplate my altar, now in Advent, with an icon of Gabriel telling Mary about the Christ child she is carrying. Here I am overwhelmed by the faithfulness of God to redeem and renew us no matter what the cost. I draw strength, confident we trust in a God who is vulnerable enough to come as a human child and dwell among us, in spite of knowing this child, this beloved Son, would be persecuted, rejected, and crucified. Throughout the biblical story, our vulnerable God is exposed to rejection and pain, revealing a trustworthiness to human welfare and flourishing that is astounding.

I continue to swivel to the candle on my desk where my thoughts go to the ways that God has lovingly guided my vocational journey. Two distinct careers—medical practice in Australia, New Zealand, and with Mercy Ships, and now as an author, blogger, and speaker. The tenderness with which God still leads me speaks of a faithfulness and trustworthiness that is beyond my comprehension. I think of the creativity and imagination that has bubbled up within me as I experiment with painting rocks, create meditation gardens, craft prayers, and contemplate the beauty of creation.

Last but not least, my attention moves to a small table with an embroidered cross displayed on it, an old cross probably created in the early twentieth century. In front are a couple of jagged crystals I picked up in Australia many years ago. This "station" speaks of God's loving faithfulness in times of struggle and pain not just in my life but throughout the ages to all the peoples of the earth.

Now my circle is complete and I sit in God's loving embrace, filled with joyful trust in a God I know has always been with me and will never leave me. God is love; God is trustworthy in the depths of my heart. I am sure of it.

TRUST GOD FROM THE BOTTOM OF YOUR HEART

On cross?

Jesus never loses his childlike trust. His infallible belief in the faithfulness of God in the face of torture and crucifixion is astounding. His

But before that . . .

final words are "Father, I entrust My spirit into Your hands!" (Luke 23:46).
Trust in and dependence on God in the midst of agony and doubt.
Perhaps it is because he never lost the childlike qualities of awe and
wonder, gratitude, compassion, and love of nature that this is possible.

Proverbs 3:5-12 explains this kind of trust.

> Trust GOD from the bottom of your heart
> > don't try to figure out everything on your own.
>
> Listen for GOD's voice in everything you do, everywhere you go;
> > he's the one who will keep you on track.
>
> Don't assume that you know it all.
> > Run to GOD! Run from evil!
>
> Your body will glow with health,
> > your very bones will vibrate with life!
>
> Honor GOD with everything you own;
> > give him the first and the best.
>
> Your barns will burst,
> > your wine vats will brim over.
>
> But don't, dear friend, resent GOD's discipline;
> > don't sulk under his loving correction.
>
> It's the child he loves that GOD corrects;
> > a father's delight is behind all this. (*The Message*)

This kind of trust reminds me of the mountains around Seattle. They
are part of what I love about the city. To the west are the beautiful
Olympic Mountains, which I see outside my office window. To the
east are the Cascades, dominated by what we call "the Mountain," Mt.
Rainier, a magnificent 15,000 ft. high peak. I never tire of its beauty,
and when I fly home from a trip, it is my first sight of this mountain
that I long for.

(Mt Rainier)

Sometimes it is completely shrouded in clouds. I have had visitors from Australia come for a week without ever glimpsing its awe-inspiring summit. They never doubt its existence though. It doesn't take much faith for them to believe that in the midst of the clouds, the majesty of enormous Mt. Rainier still rises to the glory of God.

Often, when the mountain reappears, it has changed from my last sight of it. A fresh layer of snow after a winter storm or a new, lush pasture after a summer rain. It changes with the light too. Sometimes it glows with the reds and yellows of sunrise and sunset. At night I drink in the glory of its moon-splashed image. Whatever the time or season the mountain's appearance is always spectacular.

Trusting in God is a little like believing in Mt. Rainier—enormous, magnificent, always there, always glorious but sometimes shrouded in cloud. Just as I trust that the mountain has not moved *but it has!*, even when I cannot see it, I trust that God has not moved either. This, as the writer of Hebrews tells us, is the firm foundation under everything that makes life worthwhile: "The fundamental fact of existence is that this trust in God, this faith, is the firm foundation under everything that makes life worth living. It's our handle on what we can't see. The act of faith is what distinguished our ancestors, set them above the crowd" (Hebrews 11:1-2 *The Message*).

What are the clouds that obscure God's glory for you and make it difficult to trust with childlike abandon? What new practices have you established that increased your trust in God as a result of reading this book? Reflect back on the childlike characteristics we have discussed. Reread your journal. What stands out for you?

> WHAT ARE THE CLOUDS THAT OBSCURE GOD'S GLORY FOR YOU AND MAKE IT DIFFICULT TO TRUST WITH CHILDLIKE ABANDON?

Are there ways these have made you feel more vulnerable? Are there ways they have made you more trusting?

A NEVER-ENDING JOURNEY

As I sit in my office, contemplating the journey the writing of this book has taken me on, I am reminded of Jesus' words: "I have come that they may have life, and have it to the full" (John 10:10 NIV), or as *The Message* beautifully expresses it, "I came so they can have real and eternal life, more and better life than they ever dreamed of."

Jesus came that we might have a better life than we ever dreamed of, a childlike life that ushers us into the kingdom of God. My prayer is that this book has enabled you to take steps toward that life and that you may continue to journey into the fullness of God.

PRACTICE
Braid the Cords Together

This final exercise is intended to give you something tangible to take away that will remind you to practice what you have learned.

Ecclesiastes 4:12 says, "A rope made of three strands is not quickly broken." It is my hope that through reading this book you have braided together strands of a rope of new practices that bring joy to you and to God in the process.

When Kim Balke read this braiding meditation she commented,

> I often braid my hair in the morning and now it has become a richer/deeper experience. I braid my hair because it is frizzy. The wonder of braiding it is that it helps it "relax into curls"... lovely curls, flexible curls ... each of the frizzy hairs and especially the drawing them into three thick strands, each one helps the other smooth out ... an analogy for sure to my spiritual practice of relinquishment to God ... every strand of sorrow, anxiety, misunderstanding/perplexity transforms with patience, trust and waiting on God into delight, curiosity/openness and lovingkindness.[1]

Prayerfully think about what you have read and experimented with. Which new practices are particularly meaningful for you? Perhaps you would like to braid them together into a friendship bracelet. Braiding a friendship bracelet that you wear on your wrist is one way to remind yourself of the childlike attributes that stirred your imagination and inspired you to create new practices. Or, like Kim, you might like to use this exercise to give deeper meaning to an experience that is already part of your day.

So let's get creative.[2]

Braiding the cord. You can make this bracelet with different colored yarn or jute, but it is better with braided nylon cord, like 1.4 mm

Chinese knotting cord, available at most craft stores. You will need three spools in different colors, scissors, and a lighter.

The instructions that follow are for a basic double braid.

If you want to wrap the bracelet around your wrist once, cut the cords to nineteen inches. This will give you seven inches of braiding and a five-inch tail at each end. For each additional eight inches of cord length, you get an additional seven inches of braiding. You can customize the length for wrapping around your wrist two or three times or for making book marks and decorative ribbons. This can be a fun and creative exercise with many ways to display your "rope of three strands that is not easily broken."

Cut six strands—two of each color to the length you have chosen. Put one pair of cords to the left, one in the center, and one to the right. Tie them together with a simple knot five inches from the end and tape them to a flat surface like a table or clip board. "Pull the left-hand pair over the center pair so that it becomes the center pair. . . . Pull the right-hand pair over the center pair so that it becomes the center pair." "Keep the pairs of thread flat, one strand next to the other, making sure they don't get twisted as you go. This way bracelet will lay flat when you're done."[3]

When you reach your desired length of braiding, use one of the outer strands to tie another simple overhand knot tightly twice around all the other strands. Snip the other strands very close to the knot.

"In a well-ventilated room burn the ends of these snipped strands until they melt together and are secured. Untie the knot at the beginning of the bracelet. Use an outer-edge cord to tie a knot tightly twice around all of the other cord strands, just as you did for the end of the bracelet. Snip off the cords except for the one you used to tie the knots, and burn the beginning just as you did the end."[4]

If you are making a book mark, you are done. For a bracelet, make sure the braid isn't twisted. "Tie the left-hand tail in a double knot around the right-hand tail 1 3/4 inches from the end of the braided section. Snip off the left-hand tail and burn the tail and the knot wraps together to secure the knot. . . . Repeat for the right-hand end. Your bracelet will now be complete with a closure that slides open and shut by pulling on both knots."[5]

Prayerfully contemplate your braided cord. Are there specific practices that each strand represents for you? Perhaps they remind you of childlike attributes you want to incorporate into your life. Take out your journal and write down what comes to mind. You might like to sketch your bracelet, labeling each strand with the attributes or practices it represents for you.

Wear your bracelet or use the bookmark to remind you of the new habits you are establishing. I like to hold it in my hand, fingering the different strands and reflecting on what I have learned. How else might you use it?

HAVE SOME FUN WITH FRIENDS

For your final meeting plan a party. A potluck is the easiest. Find out what each person's favorite childhood food was and try to make it or get them to bring it along as part of your feast. Decorate your meeting place with balloons and streamers. Plan some games. Encourage participants to use the braiding exercise before the party and bring their bracelets with them.

While you eat, share your bracelet stories. What new practices are you encouraged to incorporate into your lives? What new practice might you incorporate in your group?

Finish with a time of prayer, and commit yourself to God and God's kingdom purposes. You might like to use this prayer as a commitment prayer.

We arise today present with the Holy One,
    in the embrace of love,
    in the hope of renewal,
    in the joy of belonging to the great I AM.

We arise today in the life of the Creator,
    in the image of the Eternal One,
    planter of gardens, bearer of burdens,
    bringer of laughter, breath of the world.
We arise today children of the faithful One,
    lover of souls, reviver of spirits,
    blesser of all that is good,
    fun-loving, joy-filled and delightful.
We choose to live today,
    in the name of the caring One,
    compassion in our hearts,
    gratitude in our thoughts,
    generosity in our deeds,
    justice as our passion.
We choose to live today
    in the light of Christ.[6]

ACKNOWLEDGMENTS

It takes a community to write a book, and this one is no exception. So many have helped me on the journey that it is impossible for me to thank everyone, but there a few without whom this book would never have come into being.

My Facebook friends who responded enthusiastically to my question What are the childlike characteristics that make us fit for the kingdom of God? deserve a special mention. They set the trajectory for this book and led me into a world of childlike wonder and mystery I suspect I would not otherwise have discovered.

Special thanks to Mark Pierson and Lilly Lewin, who opened a whole new world to me as they encouraged my first tentative steps into creative spiritual practices and liturgical prayers. They read my evolving thoughts, suffered patiently through the early versions of my manuscript, edited content, and continued to direct and guide me as the final version took shape.

Good friends Tom and Kim Balke have also given invaluable help. Kim, an expressive arts therapist who works with children, delighted me with suggestions of childlike practices I could experiment with and has been the inspiration for many of the creative practices at the end of each chapter. Tom spent many hours painstakingly reading through each version, noticed details I never saw, corrected my grammar, and gave helpful advice and guidance on all that I wrote.

Kerry Dearborn, another longtime friend and theologian, also gave invaluable assistance, questioning my sometimes wayward assumptions and leading me to enriching resources I would otherwise not have come across.

Another huge thank you goes to my editor at InterVarsity Press, Cindy Bunch. She redirected my early ideas and helped shaped this book into something I could never have imagined.

Finally, I want to thank my husband, Tom Sine, without whom this book would never have come into being. He not only encouraged me to write what God had placed on my heart but enthusiastically embraced some of the emerging practices, like awe-and-wonder walks, that flowed out of my research. His love and support go with me every step of the way.

APPENDIX

Guidelines for Leading a Group

The Gift of Wonder is written for groups who want to explore more creative approaches to spiritual practices. The exercises at the end of each chapter have a special section titled "Have Some Fun with Friends," written to help facilitate study groups, Sunday school classes, book groups, or informal gatherings of friends interested in the topic. It is particularly appropriate for classes on spiritual formation or for use during seasons of reflection in the church calendar like Lent or Advent.

A group of eight to ten people is ideal for the following plan. If you have a larger group get participants to sit at tables (preferably circular) of eight to ten people and conduct the group activities around the table. In some sessions you might like to allow time for a representative from each table to share the most compelling suggestion their group came up with.

There are fourteen chapters in the book, and you might like to spread the study over three months, with an assigned chapter each week. A couple of the sessions could then be designated for field trips, playdates, awe-and-wonder walks, and lectio tierra reflections. Alternatively, a six-week study could be designed by combining two or three chapters for reading each week. Choose the chapter you want to focus on and one of the "at home" creative activities.

Here is a suggested format for a study group:

COME PREPARED

Ask each participant to bring a copy of *The Gift of Wonder*, their Bible, and a notebook to each session. You might also like to have them bring the toolkits they put together from the suggestions in the introduction.

In addition, group leaders should make sure that colored pencils or crayons and blank sheets of paper are available for participants to use. Consider providing templates of crosses, decorative lettering, or coloring sheets as well or ask participants to bring their own focusing tools: whittling, knitting, coloring books, journals, sketch books. If possible you might also like to provide pens and rocks to paint too. Encourage participants to use these tools throughout the session to help them both focus and reflect.

Prior to each session, encourage participants to read the designated chapters for the week. Ask them to pay particular attention to the exercise at the end of the chapter so they can come prepared for action. Make sure they are aware of any special resources they need to bring to accomplish that exercise.

DEVELOP A MEETING PLAN

I encourage you to plan sessions around a meal. A simple soup and supper or potluck are the easiest. Allow at least two hours for each session. The first few minutes of each session are spent in prayer, followed by a community-building sharing time. Allow about thirty minutes for this introduction to the session. The meat of the session is in the discussion and fun activities. Allow forty-five minutes for each of these. If you are providing a meal, an extra half hour or more is recommended so that the session does not seem hurried.

CONDUCT YOUR MEETING

Begin with prayer. Begin each session with a moment of silence. Have each person take a few deep breaths in and out to help them quiet their spirits and center on the presence of God. Recite the prayer at the beginning of the appropriate chapter and say a short prayer of your own.

Build community or show-and-tell time. Show-and-tell helps participants get to know each other better. At the first session get each person to introduce themselves and ask them, Why are you interested in studying *The Gift of Wonder*? Or you might like to start with a fun question like, How do you like to play? At subsequent sessions ask, How did last week's session affect your week? What is one fun thing you did in response? Make sure each person has time to share without interruption (if they want to). Limit responses to one or two minutes depending on the size of your group or this will take over the session.

You may even like to introduce the use of a talking stick. Any stick will do, though it is more fun if you write "Talking Stick" on it and color or decorate it before the first session. Native American tribes use talking sticks as a symbol of a person's authority to speak. This is particularly helpful if you have someone who tends to dominate the conversation. Whoever is holding the stick has the authority to talk without interruption. When they finish speaking, they either pass the stick to someone else or place it back in the center of the circle for someone to pick up. Discourage participants from responding to what others share with questions, advice, or even sympathy because this tends to take the focus away from the sharer onto the responder.

Pause for a minute between each person to allow the words to sink in. At the end, have one person say a prayer committing all you have heard to God.

Time for discussion. Discussion should revolve around the chapters designated for the session. Allow at least forty-five minutes for this part of the session. Good questions to prompt discussion are

- What did you find most helpful in your week's reading?
- What did you struggle with the most?

- What is your response to the creative suggestions in the chapter?
- What is one fun thing you would like to do next week in response to your reading?

Time to play. Activities at the end of each chapter are designed to ground the study in personal commitment and action. If you are conducting a six-week study, choose one of the exercises at the end of the chapters you have read that week. You might even like to suggest that participants experiment with other creative suggestions over the coming week and bring their creations to the next session for show-and-tell. Experience helps us learn and moves the information we have read from our heads to our hearts. Please don't skip this part of the session. Allow thirty minutes for this creativity time, and then have a time of sharing at the end. Allow at least fifteen minutes for this.

Close with prayer. At the end of the session sit quietly again as you did at the beginning. Take some deep breaths in and out, and center yourself once more on the embracing presence of God. Prayerfully consider: *What is one response God is asking of me as a result of this session?* Encourage participants to write their responses in a journal or notebook. Conclude with a prayer of thanksgiving for the session and all that you have learned.

CREATIVE PRACTICES

NOTES

INTRODUCTION

Opening poem by Christine Aroney-Sine, "I Choose to Enjoy," 2018.

[1] Stuart Brown, quoted in Sami Yanigun, "Play Doesn't End with Childhood: Why Adults Need Recess Too," *All Things Considered*, www.npr.org/sections /ed/2014/08/06/336360521/play-doesnt-end-with-childhood-why-adults -need-recess-too.

[2] Judy Brown Hull, *When You Receive a Child: Reflections on Luke 9:46-48* (St. Meinrad, IN: Abbey Press, 1980), 20.

[3] For a good description of lectio divina see Christina Valters Paintner, "The Transforming Power of Lectio Divina: A Deeper Look at the Four Movements," *Godspace*, August 24, 2011, http://godspacelight.com/2011/08/24 /the-transforming-power-of-lectio-divina-a-deeper-look-at-the-four -movements-christine-valters-paintner.

[4] Parker Palmer, *A Hidden Wholeness: The Journey Toward an Undivided Life* (San Francisco: Jossey-Bass, 2004), 54-55.

[5] Matthew Fox, *Creativity: Where the Divine and the Human Meet* (New York: Tarcher/Putman, 2002), 77.

1 DELIGHT YOURSELF IN GOD

Opening poem by Christine Aroney-Sine, "Marking the Way," 2018.

[1] Andrew Newberg and Mark Robert Waldman, *How God Changes the Brain* (New York: Ballantine Books, 2010), 4.

[2] Hans Urs von Balthasar, *Unless You Become Like This Child* (San Francisco: Ignatius Press, 1988), 27.

[3] Dalai Lama and Desmond Tutu, *The Book of Joy: Lasting Happiness in a Changing World* (New York: Penguin Random House, 2016), 59.

[4] Dalai Lama and Tutu, *Book of Joy*, 63.

[5] Abraham Joshua Heschel, *The Sabbath* (New York: Farrar, Straus & Giroux, 1951), 74.

[6]Norman Wirzba, *Food and Faith: A Theology of Eating* (Cambridge: Cambridge University Press, 2011), 32.

[7]J. Richard Middleton, *A New Heaven and a New Earth* (Grand Rapids: Baker Academic, 2014), 164.

[8]Heschel, *Sabbath*, 74.

[9]Christine Aroney-Sine, *Godspace: Time for Peace in the Rhythms of Life* (Newberg, OR: Barclay Press, 2006), 140.

PRACTICE—CHOOSE JOY

[1]A detailed explanation of the prayer of examen can be found at "The Daily Examen," IgnatianSpirituality.com, accessed August 7, 2018, www.ignatian spirituality.com/ignatian-prayer/the-examen.

2 OPEN YOURSELF TO AWE AND WONDER

Opening poem by Christine Aroney-Sine, "The Rhythm of God's World," 2018.

[1]Paul Piff and Dacher Keltner, "Why Do We Experience Awe?" *New York Times*, May 22, 2015, www.nytimes.com/2015/05/24/opinion/sunday/why -do-we-experience-awe.html?.

[2]Greg Boyle, *Barking to the Choir: The Power of Radical Kinship* (New York: Simon & Schuster, 2017), 56.

[3]Piff and Keltner, "Why Do We Experience Awe?"

[4]John Pridmore, *Playing with Icons: The Spirituality of Recalled Childhood* (Sewanee, TN: Godly Play, 2017), 37.

[5]Pridmore, *Playing with Icons*, 38.

[6]Christine Valters Paintner, *Lectio Divina: The Sacred Art* (Woodstock, VT: Skylight Pathways, 2011), xi-xii.

[7]Paintner, *Lectio Divina*, 83-84.

[8]Nancy Evans, "Walk to Jerusalem/Walk to Bethlehem," *Church Health Reader*, accessed August 10, 2018, http://chreader.org/walk-to-jerusalem.

[9]The original Book of Kells is preserved in Trinity College Dublin, Ireland. See "The Book of Kells," Trinity College Dublin, accessed August 10, 2018, www.tcd.ie/library/manuscripts/book-of-kells.php.

[10]"The Saint John's Bible," Saint John's University, accessed August 10, 2018, www.saintjohnsbible.org.

[11]For more information and photos of Balmy Alley, visit http://balmyalley .com.

[12]Christine Valters Paintner, *Eyes of the Heart: Photography as a Christian Contemplative Practice* (Notre Dame, IN: Sorin Books, 2013), 15.

3 LET YOUR LIFE SPEAK

Opening poem by Christine Aroney-Sine, "Let God's Love Speak to You," 2018.

[1]John Medina, *Brain Rules for the Aging: 10 Principles for Staying Vital, Happy and Sharp* (Seattle: Pear Press, 2017), 224.

[2]Medina, *Brain Rules for the Aging*, 233.

[3]Christine Aroney-Sine, "An Infant's Cry," 2018.

[4]Paul Hiebert, *Anthropological Reflections on Missiological Issues* (Grand Rapids: Baker, 1994), 168-69.

[5]Joyce Rupp, *The Cup of Our Life: A Guide to Spiritual Growth* (Notre Dame, IN: Ava Maria Press, 1997), 2.

4 UNLEASH YOUR INNER CHILD

Opening poem by Christine Aroney-Sine, "Release Your Inner Self," 2018.

[1]See Stuart Brown, "Play Is More Than Just Fun," TEDTalks, May 2008, www .ted.com/talks/stuart_brown_says_play_is_more_than_fun_it_s _vital.

[2]Dawn Stover, "The Mad Science of Creativity," *Scientific American Mind*, spring 2017, 83.

[3]See Charlie Hoehn, "Mass Shootings in America, and Why Men (and Boys) Keep Doing This," *BeYourself*, October 3, 2017, https://byrslf.co /thoughts-on-the-vegas-shooting-14af397cee2c.

[4]Brown, "Play Is More Than Just Fun," 83.

[5]Stuart Brown's play personalities are reviewed in Michael Monroe, "What's Your Play Personality?" *Empowered to Connect*, accessed August 13, 2018, http:// empoweredtoconnect.org/whats-your-play-personality.

[6]See Angie Fadel's website www.angiefadel.com.

[7]Adapted from Angie Fadel, "Making Archery Dreams Come True?" *Angie Fadel* (blog), October 12, 2016, www.angiefadel.com/single-post/2016/10/11 /Why-Archery. Used with permission.

[8]For more information on Godly Play see their website at www.godlyplay foundation.org.

[9]This description is adapted from "The Hertfordshire Scheme of Work for Primary Religious Education," Hertfordshire Grid for Learning, www .thegrid.org.uk/learning/re/general/documents/re_sow.pdf, 20.

[10]"What Is Godly Play?" Church Publishing, 2017, www.churchpublishing .org/contentassets/5dc3dc932dc64971a922f6554adacb32/what-is-godly -play.pdf.

[11]"To Discover Recovery: Godly Play for Alzheimer's Patients," Key Resources, February 3, 2014, www.keyhallonline.org/profiles/godly-play-discovery -recovery.

[12]The Maundy Thursday Agape Liturgy can be downloaded at the *Godspace* website: http://godspacelight.com/shop/maundy-thursday-agape-liturgy.

[13]For information on the Tongues of Fire Chili Cook-Off see http://faithepis copal.org/wp-content/uploads/2016/02/Tongues-of-Fire-2016.pdf.

[14]Lucy Moore, "Mess as Mystery," *Messy Church*, February 24, 2017, www .messychurch.org.uk/messy-blog/mess-mystery.

5 SET YOUR IMAGINATION FREE

Opening poem by Christine Aroney-Sine, "The Rhythm of Eternal Breath," 2018.

[1]Albert Einstein, "What Life Means to Albert Einstein," interviewed by George Sylvester Viereck, *Saturday Evening Post*, October 26, 1929, quoted in "Talk: Albert Einstein Quote," Wikiversity, accessed August 13, 2018, https://en.wikiversity.org/wiki/Talk:Albert_Einstein_quote.

[2]"About Ashes to Go," Ashes to Go, accessed August 13, 2018, https:// ashestogo.org/about-ashes-to-go.

[3]Mark Pierson, "Taking Worship Seriously," *Godspace*, accessed August 13, 2018, https://godspacelight.com/2011/10/13/taking-worship-seriously-by -worship-curator-mark-pierson.

[4]Adrienne Rewi, "185 Empty Chairs and a Church," *Adrienne Rewi Online*, February 24, 2017, http://adriennerewiimagines.blogspot.com/2012/02/185 -chairs-church.html.

[5]Randy Woodley, *The Harmony Tree: A Story of Healing and Community.* (Neche, ND: Friesen Press, 2016).

[6]Sybil MacBeth, *Praying in Color: Drawing a New Path to God* (Brewster, MA: Paraclete Press, 2007), 15.

[7]Ched Myer, "The Parable of Talents: A View from the Other Side," *Godspace*, May 18, 2010, http://godspacelight.com/2010/05/18/the-parable-of-the -talents-a-view-from-the-other-side.

6 GIVE YOURSELF THE GIFT OF CURIOSITY

Opening poem by Christine Aroney-Sine, "All Is a Gift from God," 2018.

[1]Casey Tygrett, *Becoming Curious: A Spiritual Practice of Asking Questions* (Downers Grove, IL: InterVarsity Press, 2017), 22.

[2]Thomas Merton, *Hagia Sophia*, in *A Thomas Merton Reader*, ed. Thomas P. McDonnell (New York: Image/Doubleday, 1974), 506.

[3]See Andy Wade, "What If? A Garden Meditation," *Godspace*, September 10, 2014, http://godspacelight.com/2014/09/10/what-it-a-garden-meditation -by-andy-wade.

[4]Thomas Merton, *Seasons of Celebration* (New York: Farrar, Straus & Giroux, 1965), 15.

[5]Dalai Lama and Desmond Tutu, *The Book of Joy: Lasting Happiness in a Changing World* (New York: Penguin Random House, 2016), 63.

[6]Rebecca Sonit, *A Paradise Built in Hell* (New York: Viking Adult, 2009), 306.

[7]John O'Donohue, *Beauty: The Invisible Embrace* (New York: HarperCollins, 2004), 225.

[8]Josh Parks, "Prayer Labyrinth Provides Space for Meditation, Prayer During Holy Week," *Chimes*, March 26, 2015, www.calvin.edu/chimes/2015/03/26 /prayer-labyrinth-provides-space-for-meditation-prayer-during-holy-week.

[9]"Labyrinth Prayer Walk for Holy Week," *Daughters of Wisdom*, March 24, 2013, www.daughtersofwisdom.org.uk/labyrinth-prayer-walk-for-holy -week/.

PRACTICE—WALK A FINGER LABYRINTH

[1]There are many places to download different labyrinth templates. Relax-4Life's "Labyrinth Resources" (relax4life.com/paperlabyrinths.html) is one I have used on several occasions.

7 REMEMBER WE ARE EARTHLINGS

Opening poem by Christine Aroney-Sine, "Deep Roots," 2018.

[1]Fred Bahnson, *Soil and Sacrament: A Spiritual Memoir of Food and Faith* (New York: Simon & Schuster, 2013), 8.

[2]Fred Bahnson and Norman Wirzba, *Making Peace with the Land: God's Call to Reconcile with Creation* (Downers Grove, IL: InterVarsity Press, 2013), 16.

[3]Richard Louv, "Nature-Deficit Disorder," Child & Nature Network, accessed September 5, 2018, www.childrenandnature.org/about/nature-deficit -disorder.

[4]Florence Williams, "This Is Your Brain on Nature," *National Geographic*, accessed August 14, 2018, www.nationalgeographic.com/magazine/2016/01 /call-to-wild.

[5]David Strayer, quoted in Williams, "This Is Your Brain on Nature."

[6]"Texas School Beats ADHD by Tripling Recess Time," *Return to Now*, November 11, 2017, https://returntonow.net/2017/11/21/texas-school -beaths-adhd-tripling-recess-time.

⁷B. Brett Finlay and Marie-Claire Arrieta, *Let Them Eat Dirt: How Microbes Can Make Your Child Healthier*, repr. ed. (New York: Algonquin Books, 2017).

⁸John O'Donohue, *Beauty: The Invisible Embrace* (New York: HarperCollins, 2004), 140.

⁹O'Donohue, *Beauty*, 141.

¹⁰J. Philip Newell, *Christ of the Celts* (San Francisco: Jossey-Bass, 2008), 50.

¹¹Simple instructions can be found at Kristen Welch's blog, http://wearethatfamily.com/2012/03/diy-mini-resurrection-garden.

¹²Christine Aroney-Sine, "A Garden Blessing," in *To Garden with God* (Seattle: Mustard Seed Associates, 2009), 109.

¹³This exercise is adapted from Andy Wade, "Listening to the Life of Jesus . . . in a Tree," *Godspace*, August 25, 2016, http://godspacelight.com/2016/08/25/listening-to-the-life-of-jesus-in-a-tree.

¹⁴For a rich array of Earth Day resources visit A Rocha Canada's "Good Seed Sunday," website at https://arocha.ca/get-involved/good-seed-Sunday.

¹⁵For great instructions on how to make seed bombs, see "How to Make a Seed Bomb," WikiHow, www.wikihow.com/Make-a-Seed-Bomb.

¹⁶"Resources: Church Resources," Operation Noah, accessed August 15, 2018, http://operationnoah.org/resources/how-green-is-your-church-audit-questionnaire.

8 RETURN TO THE RHYTHM OF LIFE
Opening poem by Christine Aroney-Sine, "God of Rhythm and Balance," 2018.

¹Ray S. Anderson, *The Seasons of Hope: Empowering Faith Through the Practice of Hope* (Eugene, OR: Wipf & Stock, 2008), 9.

²For more information on the work that Mary and to see some of her mandala designs see the Waymarkers website: www.waymarkers.net.

³This reflection is adapted from a blog post I wrote several years ago: Christine Aroney-Sine, "Weathering the Winter Storms—Lessons for the Soul," *Godspace*, January 23, 2012, http://godspacelight.com/2012/01/23/weathering-the-winter-storms-lessons-for-the-soul.

⁴Christine Aroney-Sine, "The Seeds of Life," 2018.

9 REST IN THE MOMENT
Opening poem by Christine Aroney-Sine, "The Moment of God's Creating," 2018.

¹Ann Voskamp, *One Thousand Gifts: A Dare to Live Fully Right Where You Are* (Grand Rapids: Zondervan, 2011), 74.

[2]Christine Aroney-Sine, "The Breath of God," in "A Breathing Prayer," *Godspace*, February 16, 2009, https://godspacelight.com/2009/02/16/a-breathing-prayer.

[3]Christine Aroney-Sine, "Breathing Room for My Soul," 2018.

[4]John O'Donahue, *The Four Elements* (London: Transworld Ireland, 1995), xxix.

[5]Christine Aroney-Sine, "Welcome the Triune God," 2018.

[6]"The Daily Awareness Examen," Imago Dei Christian Community, December 5, 2005, https://imagodeicommunity.ca/category/awareness-examen.

[7]Rodney Newman, *Journeys with Celtic Christians* (Nashville: Abingdon, 2015), 70.

[8]Ian Bradley, *The Celtic Way* (London: Darton, Longman and Todd, 2003), 47.

[9]See my "House Blessing," in "Prayer for the Season—A House Blessing," *Godspace*, August 19, 2015, http://godspacelight.com/2015/08/19/prayer-for-the-week-a-house-blessing.

[10]Christine Aroney-Sine, "Circle Us, Lord," 2018.

[11]Christine Aroney-Sine, "Circle Me," 2018.

10 CULTIVATE GRATITUDE

Opening poem by Christine Aroney-Sine, "Thank You, Lord," 2018.

[1]Janice Kaplan, *The Gratitude Diaries: How a Year Looking on the Bright Side Can Transform Your Life* (New York: Penguin Random House, 2015), 13.

[2]Kaplan, *Gratitude Diaries*, 13.

[3]Kaplan, *Gratitude Diaries*, 16.

[4]Hans Urs von Balthasar, *Unless You Become Like This Child* (San Francisco: Ignatius Press, 1991), 48-49.

[5]Balthasar, *Unless You Become Like This Child*, 49.

[6]Matthew Fox, *Creativity: Where the Divine and the Human Meet* (New York: Jeremy P. Tarcher/Putman, 2002), 24.

[7]Sue Duby, "What Do We Hunger and Thirst For?" *Godspace*, February 25, 2012, http://godspacelight.com/2012/02/25/what-do-we-hunger-thirst-for-by-sue-duby.

[8]Duby, "What Do We Hunger and Thirst For?"

[9]"Gratitude," Edison Township School District Newsletter, December 20, 2015, www.edison.k12.nj.us/cms/lib2/NJ01001623/Centricity/Domain/2034/December%202015%20-%20Gratitude.doc.

[10]Robert Emmons, "Ten Ways to Become More Grateful," *Greater Good*, November 17, 2010, https://greatergood.berkeley.edu/article/item/ten_ways_to_become_more_grateful1.

[11]"Delicious Dinner Rolls Recipe," *How Does She?* October 15, 2016, https://howdoesshe.com/delicious-dinner-rolls.

[12]Jason Marsh, "Tips for Keeping a Gratitude Journal," *Greater Good*, November 17, 2011, https://greatergood.berkeley.edu/article/item/tips_for_keeping_a_gratitude_journal.

[13]Christine Aroney-Sine, "Thank You, Lord, for You," 2018.

[14]Christine Aroney-Sine, "Bless God for Seasons," 2018.

[15]*Guided gratitude interventions* is a term I picked up from "31 Gratitude Exercises That Will Boost Your Happiness (+PDF)," Positive Psychology Program, April 28, 2017, https://positivepsychologyprogram.com/gratitude-exercises/#interventions.

[16]Emmons, *Ten Ways to Become More Grateful.*

PRACTICE—PLAN A GRATITUDE SCAVENGER HUNT

[1]This list is adapted from "Gratitude Photo Scavenger Hunt," *Let's Get Together*, October 18, 2014, https://lets-get-together.com/2014/10/18/gratitude-photo-scavenger-hunt.

11 SEE THINGS DIFFERENTLY

Opening poem by Christine Aroney-Sine, "Listen," 2018.

[1]You can view the video on YouTube: "Everyone's Welcome," Cbeebies, June 17, 2017, https://youtu.be/1MJrRvpjB1I.

[2]This reflection is adapted from my blog post "Meditation Monday: The Woman with the Perfume," *Godspace*, July 6, 2015, http://godspacelight.com/2015/07/06/meditation-monday-the-woman-with-the-perfume.

[3]This quote evidently comes from Marcel Proust's *La Prisonnière*, the fifth volume of Remembrance of Things Past. However, it is much quoted on the internet. See, for example, "Marcel Proust Quotes," *Brainy Quote*, accessed September 5, 2018, www.brainyquote.com/quotes/marcel_proust_107111.

[4]John O'Donohue, *Beauty: The Invisible Embrace* (New York: HarperCollins, 2005), 28.

[5]Lesslie Newbigin, *Foolishness to the Greeks* (Grand Rapids: Eerdmans, 1986), 146.

[6]See Matt Stone's *Curious Christian* blog, https://curiouschristian.blog.

[7]See He Qi's art gallery on his new website: www.heqiart.com.

[8]See "'Jesus Mafa' Paintings," *Indigenous Jesus*, December 14, 2011, http://indigenousjesus.blogspot.com/2011/12/jesus-mafa-paintings.html.

[9]"Iraq War Stations of the Cross to Go on View at L.A.," *Cision*, December 20, 2005, www.prweb.com/releases/2005/12/prweb324049.htm.

[10]Adolfo Pérez Esquivel, "Stations of the Cross from Latin America 1492-1992," Alistair McIntosh.com, December 23, 2005, www.alastair mcintosh.com/general/1992-stations-cross-esquivel.pdf.

[11]"The Stations of the Cross—An Original Interpretation," Radio Praha, accessed August 17, 2018, http://old.radio.cz/en/html/easter05_cesta.html.

[12]See the Global Christian Worship website at http://globalworship.tumblr.com.

[13]"Advent Activity Tree," *The Imagination Tree*, November 28, 2011, https://theimaginationtree.com/advent-activity-tree.

[14]"Christmas Around the World," Why Christmas? accessed August 17, 2018, www.whychristmas.com/cultures.

[15]Emma Morgan, "Advent Nativity Activity—Santons in the Home and Church," *Godspace*, Nobember 28, 2014, https://godspace-msa.com/2014/11/28/advent-nativity-activity-santons-in-the-home-and-church-by-emma-morgan.

[16]This account is adapted from "The Cross of St George," Barnabas in Churches, accessed August 17, 2018, www.barnabasinchurches.org.uk/the-cross-of-st-george, which also contains an excellent children's activity reflecting on St. George and his significance to Palestinian Christians.

PRACTICE—MAKE A RAINBOW

[1]John O'Donohue, *Beauty: The Invisible Embrace* (New York: HarperCollins, 2004), 85.

[2]The rainbow maker instructions are adapted from Sue Lively, "How to Make Rainbows at Home," *One Time Through*, February 26, 2015, http://onetime through.com/how-to-make-rainbows-at-home.

[3]"Holy Week Art from Cameroon (Jesus Mafa)," Global Christian Worship, March 1, 2016, http://globalworship.tumblr.com/post/140296566140/holy-week-art-from-cameroon-jesus-mafa; "He Qi Art Gallery," HeQiArt.com, www.heqiart.com; and "Our Nativity Collection," World Nativity, accessed August 17, 2018, www.worldnativity.com/our-collection.html.

[4]Lesslie Newbigin, *Foolishness to the Greeks* (Grand Rapids: Eerdmans, 1986), 146.

12 STAY CLOSE TO THE CRACKS

Opening poem by Christine Aroney-Sine, "Stay Close to the Cracks," 2018.

[1]Stacey Kennelly, "What Motivates Kids to Help Others?" *Greater Good*, June 19, 2012, https://greatergood.berkeley.edu/article/item/what_motivates _kids_to_help_others.

[2]Leonard Cohen, "Anthem," *The Future*, Columbia, 1992.

[3]Greg Boyle, *Barking to the Choir: The Power of Radical Kinship* (New York: Simon & Schuster, 2017), 56.

[4]Tertullian, *Apology*, chap. 39, sec. 7.

[5]Evelyn Heard, "Faith," *The Age*, October 13, 2017, www.theage.com.au /victoria/faith-20171013-gz0ik1.html.

[6]See The Carasa Foundation, Facebook, accessed August 20, 2018, www .facebook.com/theCARASAfoundation.

[7]"Meet the Founder," Kindness Rocks Project, accessed September 5, 2018, www.thekindnessrocksproject.com/meet-the-founder.

[8]See the Compassion Games website at http://compassiongames.org.

[9]Brad Aronson, "103 Random Acts of Kindness—Ideas to Inspire Kindness," *Brad Aronson* (blog), accessed August 20, 3018, www.bradaronson.com /acts-of-kindness.

[10]Katie Metzger, "Fashion and Ethics: Why Should I Care and What Can I Do?" *Godspace*, accessed August 31, 2018, https://godspacelight.com /2015/04/14/fashion-and-ethics.

[11]Greg Valerio, "Fairtrade God Uganda: An Answer to Prayer," *Greg Valerio* (blog), accessed August 20, 2018, https://gregvalerio.com/featured/fairtrade -gold-uganda-an-answer-to-prayer.

13 COME TO THE TABLE

Opening poem by Christine Aroney-Sine, "Welcome, Lord," 2018.

[1]Moriah Balingit, "1 in 10 Young Adults Has Been Homeless Over the Past Year, Survey Finds," *Washington Post*, December 31, 2017, www.washingtonpost.com /local/education/one-in-ten-youth-have-been-homeless-over-the-past-year -survey-finds/2017/12/31/6acfcef2-ebf7-11e7-8a6a-80acf0774e64_story.html?.

[2]Henri Nouwen, *Reaching Out: The Three Movements of the Spiritual Life* (New York: Doubleday, 1986), 79.

[3]Nouwen, *Reaching Out*, 82.

[4]Norman Wirzba, *Food and Faith: A Theology of Eating* (Cambridge: Cambridge University Press, 2011), 11.

[5]Kendall Vanderslice, "Dinner Churches Spring Up Nationwide," Christian Food Movement, January 13, 2017, http://christianfoodmovement.org/2017 /01/13/dinner-churches-spring-up-nationwide.

[6]Vanderslice, "Dinner Churches Spring Up Nationwide."

[7]See the *Community Dinners* website at www.communitydinners.com.

[8]See the *Potluck Church* website at www.potluckchurch.com.

[9]Kenneth Bailey, *Jesus Through Middle Eastern Eyes* (Downers Grove, IL: IVP Academic, 2008), 34.

[10]This paragraph is adapted from Christine Aroney-Sine, "Stable, Inn or Welcoming Home—Where Was Jesus Born and Why Does It Matter?" *Godspace*, December 1, 2013, http://godspacelight.com/2013/12/01/stable-inn -or-welcoming-home-where-was-jesus-born-and-why-does-it-matter.

14 EMBRACE TRUST

Opening poem by Christine Aroney-Sine, "Draw Your Circle, Lord," 2018.

PRACTICE—BRAID THE CORDS TOGETHER

[1]Kim Balke, email to author, January 11, 2018.

[2]This exercise is adapted from "Braided Friendship Bracelets," Purl Soho, accessed August 20, 2018, www.purlsoho.com/create/2013/06/27/mollys -sketchbook-braided-friendship-bracelets. At this website you will find more detailed instructions along with photos.

[3]"Braided Friendship Bracelets," Purl Soho.

[4]"Braided Friendship Bracelets," Purl Soho.

[5]"Braided Friendship Bracelets," Purl Soho.

[6]Christine Aroney-Sine, "We Arise Today," 2018.

formatio

TRADITION. EXPERIENCE.
TRANSFORMATION.

Formatio books from InterVarsity Press follow the rich tradition of the church in the journey of spiritual formation. These books are not merely about being informed, but about being transformed by Christ and conformed to his image. Formatio stands in InterVarsity Press's evangelical publishing tradition by integrating God's Word with spiritual practice and by prompting readers to move from inward change to outward witness. InterVarsity Press uses the chambered nautilus for Formatio, a symbol of spiritual formation because of its continual spiral journey outward as it moves from its center. We believe that each of us is made with a deep desire to be in God's presence. Formatio books help us to fulfill our deepest desires and to become our true selves in light of God's grace.